W9-AHF-603

Also available from Continuum:

Chinese Religion: A Contextual Approach, Xinzhong Yao and Yanxia Zhao

Forthcoming:

Classical Chinese Philosophy: An Introduction, Manyul Im

Reading the *Dao*

A Thematic Inquiry

Keping Wang

continuum

Continuum International Publishing Group

The Tower Building   80 Maiden Lane
11 York Road   Suite 704
London SE1 7NX   New York, NY 10038

www.continuumbooks.com

© Keping Wang, 2011

All rights reserved. No part of this publication may be reproduced or
transmitted in any form or by any means, electronic or mechanical,
including photocopying, recording, or any information storage or retrieval
system, without prior permission in writing from the publishers.

British Library Cataloguing-in-Publication Data
A catalogue record for this book is available from the British Library.

ISBN: HB: 978–1–4411–8611–9
         PB: 978–1–4411–9651–4

Library of Congress Cataloging-in-Publication Data
Wang, Keping, 1955–
Reading the *Dao*: a thematic inquiry/Keping Wang.
p. cm.
   Includes bibliographical references.
   ISBN-13: 978–1–4411–8611–9
   ISBN-10: 1–4411–8611–5
   ISBN-13: 978–1–4411–9651–4 (pbk.)
   ISBN-10: 1–4411–9651–X (pbk.)
   1. Laozi. Dao De Jing. I. Title.
BL1900.L35W333 2010
299.5'1482—dc22
                                   2010018295

Typeset by RefineCatch Limited, Bungay, Suffolk
Printed and bound in India by Replika Press Pvt Ltd

The *Dao* in early Daoism is assumed to be the right way or path along which its practitioners are walking in their lifetime journeys and heading for their sound destinations. This is said accordingly to help transform them into truly self-contented and wise beings. According to Laozi, however,

'When the highest type of *literati* hear of the *Dao*,
  They diligently practice it.
When the average type of *literati* hear of the *Dao*,
  They half-believe it.
When the lowest type of *literati* hear of the *Dao*,
  They laugh heartily at it.
If they did not laugh at it,
  It would not be the *Dao*.'

Contents

Acknowledgements

Recent years witnessed the plurality of Confucian colleges springing up across the world. Even though most of them are basically oriented towards language learning, they are intended to help the clients get acquainted with Chinese cultural heritage for sure. To my mind, this heritage is actually characterized with a complementary relationship between Confucianism and Daoism (Taoism). These two schools of thought are claimed to represent two value systems: one is kinetic and moralistic with social commitment as is demonstrated in Confucianism, while the other static and spiritual with social detachment as is perceived in Daoism. They seem therefore to form the mainstream structure of the *Yang* and the *Yin*, or the explicit and the implicit, serving to affect and develop the Chinese way of thinking and mental state as well. It is for this reason that one who wants to know more about Chinese tradition needs to read about both the Confucian and Daoist classics. For this and many other purposes, a lot of writings are produced in Chinese, especially since the archeological findings of the Mawangdui versions of such classics on silk in 1973 and that of the Guodian versions of such canons on bamboo slips in 1993. Indebted to these contributions in this regard, the book of mine is written for the readers overseas rather than those at home.

Hence I am grateful to those who are preoccupied with the archeological research relating to the Laozi scholarship. Their fruitful work has clarified many skeptical issues with respect to Laozi and his book. Moreover, it provides a solid ground to rediscover the philosophizing of early Daoism.

I am equally grateful to many Laozi scholars who have advanced this sphere of study by means of their substantial investigation of the text of the *Dao De Jing* (*Tao-Te Ching* or *The Way and Its Power*). There are so many of them ranging through the history of over two millennia in China. Here I would like to mention only a few of the leading and contemporary ones, including Gu Di and Zhou Ying who are co-authors of the *Laozi tong* (*A Comprehensive Study of the Dao De Jing of Laozi*), and Chen Guying who is the editor of the *Laozi zhuyi ji pinglie* (*The Dao De Jing of Laozi Annotated and Commented*). The two books are virtually encyclopedias of Laozi studies at the present-day stage. As for the English rendering of the *Dao De Jing* (DDJ) itself, it owes a great deal to what has been done before by such scholars as Wing-tsit Chan, Robert G. Henricks, Arthur Waley, D.C. Lau, Richard John Lynn, and He Guanghu, among others.

I am particularly grateful to Sarah Campbell, Tom Crick, Donna White, and their colleagues from Continuum Press for their interest in this project and their unflagging assistance involved. The publication of this book will facilitate an easy accessibility for a much wider scope of international readership. This may lead to an effective scrutiny and intercultural exploration of the practical wisdom in early Daoism as is exemplified in the *Dao De Jing* (DDJ).

Finally, I would like to take this occasion to extend my heartfelt thanks to Professors Li Zehou (Colorado), Cheng Chung-ying (Hawaii), Nicholas Bunnin (Oxford), David Cooper (Durham), Richard Lynn (Toronto), Rick Benitez (Sydney), Kevin Brien (Washington), Robert Wilkinson (Edinburgh), and some of my Chinese colleagues here in Beijing for their encouragement, advice, and support in varied ways prior to and during the writing of this book. In addition, I still cherish all the good memories of late Professor Mainusch and Dr Servomaa who were so enthusiastic about Daoist ideas concerning art creation, but unfortunately left us so early at a time when we were planning to collaborate in this domain of research. Thus, I am always feeling obliged to do something more in this regard.

Preface

According to the hitherto archeological and research findings in China, the keystone of early Daoism claims to be largely embodied in the two versions under the given heading of *The Book of Laozi*: one is the Guodian version on bamboo slips that is composed of over 2000 words, and the other is the Mawangdui version on silk that is composed of over 5000 words. The latter is said to stem from the former, but further extended and enriched by taking in some ideas from other sources including the School of Military Strategists (*Bingjia*) and Legalism (*Fajia*), among others (Guo, 2001: 517–24; Yin, 2001: 7–12).

Nowadays the popular Taoist classic that corresponds in content to the latter version is known as the *Dao De Jing* by the ascribed author of Laozi, an older contemporary of Confucius (551–479 BC), who lived in the waning phase of the Spring and Autumn Period (841–476 BC) in Chinese history, and considered to be the founder of Daoism either as philosophy (*daojia*) or as religion (*daojiao*). As is read in the text, Laozi contemplates the way of human existence and praxis from varied perspectives, and expresses his sharp observations through suggestive and ambiguous aphorisms that seem in a stylistic sense somewhat tantamount to *The Fragments* by Heraclites.

As can be observed, the *Dao De Jing* is a synthesis of poetry, philosophical speculation, and mystical reflection. Its vague and cryptic character increases its level of difficulty for reading comprehension. In other words, the Daoist classic as such could not be read more efficiently without relevant annotations and comments. Actually ever since its emergence in the sixth century BC, there have been in Chinese history hundreds of Laozi scholars working on it via annotation and commentary. It is said that up till the Yuan Dynasty (1279–1368) there were over 3000 annotated versions of the *Dao De Jing* itself (Zhu, 2007: 1). No Chinese classics other than this one can claim such a record of scholarship. According to the recent statistics, most of the versions are lost, but some 350 of them are extant, aside from some 350 of them left in fragments. As for the number of its English translations, it is alleged to be over 100 so far.

It is noteworthy that the whole text of the *Dao De Jing* is composed of 81 sections according to the conventional arrangement, each addressing either similar or discrepant topics with as much intriguing as interweaving features. All this strikes many modern readers as a kind of verbal labyrinth in which one may get obsessed in a play of intelligence while shuffling back and forth in order to find a way out. It is mainly due to this fact that I have adopted a thematic approach to the text on the one hand, and on the other, I have prepared necessary annotations of the key notions and offered relevant comments on the basic themes. Such efforts are shown in *The Classic of the Dao: A New Investigation* that was written during mid-1990s and eventually published in 1998. It is in the Preface to this book that I have briefly described some of the reasons why I tackled the project in the manner as follows:

1   Laozi wrote the book in a poetic style based on metaphors and an expressive form of aphorisms such that many of his ideas appear to be engagingly suggestive, polysemous, and somewhat ambiguous rather than articulate. Thus, elaborate annotation and extended commentary are necessary for the reader to attain a justified comprehension and interpretation. As regards the straightforward translation of the book, as many English renderings are, it seems to me as though a glass of fine wine has been mixed with water, reducing it to a less tasteful cocktail.

2   It is largely due to the favorable cultural policy introduced since China embarked on the reform policy that the studies of Laozi and his like have made far more progress than ever before. But most of the latest achievements in this field are missing from the versions of the *Dao De Jing* available in English and other Western languages. This edition is intended to fill this gap.

3   Most English versions tend to employ ready-made terms to translate the ideas of Laozi, which I find most likely to lead the reader onto the beaten track of the occidental cultural background when it comes to cognizing what the author is supposed to say. In this case I have ventured to translate the key concepts with newly coined terminology, followed by relevant explanation. I sincerely hope that this approach will help the reader better identify what is really meant, in line with textual and contextual analysis.

4   Previously mentioned, this version of the *Dao De Jing* is *thematically* arranged in an attempt to facilitate a practical and fruitful reading today. The thematic arrangement as such is based not merely on the scrutiny of Laozi's philosophizing as a systematic whole, but also on considerations of the reading habits of the English reader. The overall aim is to obtain a more relevant understanding and effective communication with regard to the text.

5   As can be discerned in the annotations and comments provided in the current book, what we are trying to do in most cases is to attempt to gain new insights through reviewing the old text, say, to enable the reader to rediscover the relevance and significance of Laozi's way of thought in view of the contemporary socio-cultural context.

6   The present approach to the *Dao De Jing* is largely grounded on the conviction that it will be of more advantage to the reader to be directly involved in textual reading and analysis rather than to take a detour by tackling merely second-hand interpretation or reinterpretation. For it is often the case that an idiosyncratic interpreter, conceived of his own authority, gallops ahead while neglecting the reader's initiative and observation (Wang, 1998: ii–iii).

As luck would have it, this approach has been proved helpful and rewarding to a certain extent with respect to the book mentioned here. I have so far received a considerable amount of positive feedback along with interesting queries about it. Besides, the book itself is, as I was told, used as one of supplementary references and teaching materials in some institutions at home and abroad. This encourages me to shape it into a more concise version for a broader readership worldwide, who would expect to have a more smooth reading experience without being interrupted by the annotations dotted with Chinese characters as are spelt out in Latinized *pinyin* system. As a result, it leads me to chop off the annotations for the purpose and also cancel out the appendixes according to the length required. However, I have modified the structure of the book and some of the comments by adding or reducing what I think is needed. I sincerely hope this will again help enhancing more interest in exploring the practical wisdom and thought-provoking or provocative ideas in Laozi.

Reference key

DDJ = The *Dao De Jing* (*Tao-Te Ching* or *The Way and Its Power*)

   This version of reference is largely based on recent studies of the *Dao De Jing* made by Chinese scholars since the discovery of the Mawangdui copies on silk in 1973 and that of the Guodian copies on bamboo slips in 1993.

Chapter 1

The Essence of the Dao

Laozi was the first to coin the special concept of the *Dao* (*Tao*), which in turn serves as the keystone of his Daoism *qua* philosophy. Subtle and profound, the *Dao* is viewed as the origin of Heaven and Earth, and the mother of all things. It thus features a principle of all individual principles, and a movement of dialectic characteristics. In addition, there is a distinction made between the *Dao* of Heaven (*tian dao*) and the *Dao* of human (*ren dao*) that produce a highly enlightening interaction. The exposition of the *Dao* reveals Laozi's doctrine of the origin of the universe on the one hand, and his philosophy of 'following the way of spontaneity' on the other. Being-within-form (*You*) and Being-without-form (*Wu*) are described as two essential aspects of the *Dao* from which its subtlety, profundity, and dynamic potency can be apprehended accordingly. The nature of the *Dao* is a topic which runs throughout the text of the DDJ, particularly in Sections 1, 4, 6, and 25.

1.1 (Section 1)

The *Dao* that can be told is not the constant *Dao*.
The Name that can be named is not the constant Name.
The Being-without-form is the origin of Heaven and Earth;
The Being-within-form is the mother of the myriad Things.
Therefore it is always from the Being-without-form
 That the subtlety of the *Dao* can be contemplated;
Similarly it is always from the Being-within-form
 That the manifestation of the *Dao* can be perceived.
These two have the same source but different names,
 They both may be called deep and profound.
The deepest and most profound
 Is the doorway to all subtleties.

Commentary

The Chinese concept of the *Dao* literally means 'way,' 'road,' or 'path.' Based on this primary meaning, it assumed in ancient times the metaphorical sense of the 'Way of man,' signifying human morality, conduct, or truth, with its significance confined to social and human affairs. Yet in Laozi's terminology, it is found ascribed to certain metaphysically extended implications that vary with different contexts with regard to his doctrine of the origin of Heaven and Earth (i.e. universe or nature as a whole), and to the general law of natural change, social development, and ethical conduct as well.

As Han Feizi (c. 280–233 BC) defined it, the *Dao* is the total of all principles whereby all things become what they are. Such principles are the concrete rules that make each thing come into being, whereas the *Dao* is that whereby all things become complete. Therefore the *Dao* is also said to be what produces individual principles by virtue of which one thing cannot be the other. All things have their own different principles while the *Dao* brings the principles of all things into uniform agreement (Han, 1984: 1259–60).

The *Dao*, as a philosophical concept initially put forth by Laozi, carries two basic meanings: it sometimes indicates the substance of the physical world, that is, the *noumenon* of the universe, but in most cases it means the universal law that governs the motion and change of nature or reality. These two aspects tend to be so much entangled in Laozi's notion that the character of the *Dao* gets confused with its manifestation.

It is also argued that the idea of the *Dao* in the DDJ is developed from the notion of Fate (*ming*) in the pantheism prevailing since the Spring and Autumn Period (770–476 BC) in Chinese history. Fate was the negation of the concepts of Heaven (*tian*) and Spirits (*gui*) available in the religious idealism of the past. As a result of denying the existence of God with will and personality and other deities and spirits, there was no longer any master of the universe. Hence the ancient thinkers had to look beyond Heaven and Spirits for another lord to govern the cosmic order in general and all human changes in particular. Thus there emerged the theory of Fate as reflected in the pantheism. The notion of the *Dao* was thus based on the further abstraction of the theory of Fate, which can be seen as a natural product of the developmental process of thoughts experienced by the ancient Chinese thinkers.

As a result, the *Dao* is also considered as the highest category of Laozi's philosophy. Reading through the DDJ as a whole, we find that the *Dao* has five distinct meanings: (1) the undifferentiated primitive state; (2) the motion of nature; (3) the proto-material; (4) invisibility to human eyes and imperceptibility to other sense organs; and (5) the law of all things. However, Laozi himself has not yet the capacity to understand matter in general. Therefore, he puts forward the concept of undifferentiated (chaos) in his philosophical conception. The undifferentiated cannot be named: It is thus called namelessness or simplicity (Ren, 1993: 4–5).

By means of substantial research into Laozi's way of thinking, and taking account of many other individual findings by Chinese scholars, Chen Guying has reached the conclusion that the *Dao* is characterized by several denotations in specific contexts. He consequently classifies the *Dao* as the primordial natural force that contains infinite potentiality and creativity, as the metaphysical reality existent in some cases, as the universal law of things in other places, and lastly as the underlying rule or standard of human conduct and personal cultivation under certain circumstances. The *Dao* as presented in Section 1 is indescribable and unnamable. It is also formless and imageless even though it has a real existence and dynamically serves as the beginning of the universe (Chen, 1992: 4–14).

Talking about the *Dao* in his own words, Laozi proclaims first of all that language as an instrument for communication is rather limited in terms of its expressiveness. Thus he concludes that 'the *Dao* that can be told is not the constant *Dao*.' It is noteworthy that this observation could date back more than 2500 years. Historically speaking, it has generated a continuous impact on the development of Chinese theories, experiences and artistic creation in general. This can be testified to, for instance, such conceptions as 'It can be perceived but not communicated,' 'Words are forgotten when implications are obtained; implications are abandoned when imagery is realized,' 'All the significance and aura are achieved without writing down a single word,' 'Try to get hold of the inner spirit and go beyond the external shape,' and so on. Hence the notion that any verbal language is limited in expression tends to influence the Chinese way of thinking in general, and that of contemplating artworks in particular. These hidden influences will be further clarified as our scrutiny and discussion of the text moves ahead.

In spite of his assertion that 'the *Dao* that can be told is not the constant *Dao*,' Laozi still wrote more than 5000 words in a poetic form to present his ponderings on and expounding of the *Dao* as a key notion in his philosophizing. In his book, the *Dao* has always to be understood in its specific context. It contains such categories of meanings as follows:

1   The proto-material or substance which constitutes the universe;
2   The potential driving force that creates all things;
3   The underlying law related to the motion and development of all things; and
4   The standard or code with which to measure human conduct.

The *Dao* generalized in Section 1 has a double significance. It is so subtle and profound that it is indescribable in any ready-made words. It functions as the ultimate beginning of Heaven and Earth, and as the original source of the myriad things, due to its infinite potential and creativity. As a matter of fact, the flourishing and transforming of everything between Heaven and Earth merely manifest the continuous working of the *Dao* as such.

Being-without-form (*Wu*) and Being-within-form (*You*) signify two aspects of the *Dao* in Laozi's mind. They are employed to demonstrate a dynamic process of the *Dao* from its invisible state toward its visible state. The interrelationship between these two facets seems analogically identical to that between name and object or thinking and being.

Accordingly, Being-without-form is claimed to be of inexhaustible and yet invisible vitality, and encompass endless and numerous Being-within-form. The interaction between them exemplifies the process of engendering Heaven, Earth and the myriad things. As a consequence, this seemingly transcendental *Dao* comes into close contact with the phenomenal world. That is why it is deemed to bear a 'double character' which is somewhat metaphysical on the one hand, and physical on the other.

As has been observed, Section 1 (DDJ) attempts to explain the *Dao* as something beyond verbal expression and conceptualization, and that it is the origin of Heaven, Earth and all things. Many people are under the impression that Laozi's statement is deliberately mystifying when he calls the *Dao* 'deep and profound.' In fact what Laozi is stressing here is that the *Dao*, as the fountainhead of the myriad things, lies in the deep and profound origin of the universe. Although Laozi proclaimed that the *Dao* can not be named or told, he actually assures certain features of the *Dao*, for instance, namelessness and formlessness. Later in Section 25 (DDJ) Laozi further explains the essence of the *Dao* by admitting that something existed prior to Heaven and Earth, but whatever it was, it was in a state of chaos. As there was no name available for it, he called it the *Dao* for the sake of convenience. According to some scholars, Laozi made use of many terms from the empirical world to interpret the *Dao*, but then discarded them one after another. This indicates that empirical terms are inadequate for defining the *Dao*, and underlines the subtlety of the *Dao* with regard to its function.

Moreover, the concept of the *Dao* as fashioned by Laozi may have been derived from two pre-existing terms known as *tian dao* (the *Dao* of Heaven) and *tian ming* (Heavenly destiny), which seem to be associated with primitive shamanism. Laozi's concept of the *Dao* may have been a substitution for a supernatural God that used to be worshiped by the ancient Chinese. This may explain one of the reasons why religion in a divine sense has been virtually absent from the Chinese cultural tradition ever since.

To my mind, a sound comprehension of the *Dao* can hardly be possible without examining the writings of another notable Daoist thinker Zhuangzi (Chuangtzu). Unlike his predecessor Laozi who expresses his vision of the *Dao* in a highly condensed aphoristic style, Zhuangzi strives to explain his conception of the *Dao* along with its characteristics through metaphoric prose. Through his mouthpiece named *No Beginning* (Wushi) is one of his explanations given below: As the *Dao* cannot be heard, what can be heard is not the *Dao*. As the *Dao* cannot be seen, what can be seen is not the *Dao*. As the *Dao* cannot be spoken of, what can be spoken of is not the *Dao*. Do you know that what creates the form is formless? The *Dao* should not be given a name (Wang, 1999: 377–8). This is obviously an extended explication of the *Dao* as it is presented in Section 14 (DDJ).

A subsequent statement made by Zhuangzi can be counted as a further explanation. That is, 'He who, when asked about the *Dao*, gives an answer does not understand the *Dao*. And he who asks about the *Dao* has not really heard the *Dao* explained. The *Dao* is not to be asked about, and even if it is asked about, there can be no answer. To ask about what cannot be asked about is to ask for the sky (meaning to try to measure the immeasurable, such as the sky). To answer what cannot be answered is to try to split hairs. If the hair-splitter waits for the sky-asker, they neither will ever perceive the time and space that surround them on the outside, or understand the Great Beginning that is within. Such men can never trek across the Kunlun Mountains (the most formidable range of mountains known to the ancient Chinese and often cited metaphorically to suggest something sublime or extremely difficult), can never wander in the Great Void (meaning here the universe)' (Watson, 1968: 243–4). This apparently emphasizes the subtlety, profundity and indescribability of the *Dao*. However, it goes to extremes by absolutizing and mystifying these features. If the above is the case, how could it be possible for Laozi to write more than 5000 words about it? And correspondingly, how could it be possible for Daoism as a school of thought to have lodged itself permanently as a quintessential part of Chinese philosophy?

Many philosophers, both Chinese and non-Chinese, have ever since endeavored to comprehend the nature and character of the *Dao*. It is intriguing to notice that another answer to the question as to what the nature of the *Dao* is offered in Zhuangzi's work (*Geng-sang chu*). It goes like this: 'It (the *Dao*) comes from no source; it goes back in through no aperture. It has reality, yet there is no place where it resides. It has duration, yet no beginning or end. Something emerges, though through no aperture – this refers to the fact that it has reality. It has reality, yet there is no place where it resides – this refers to the dimension of space. It has duration, but no beginning or end – this refers to the dimension of time. There is life, there is death, there is a coming out, there is a going back in – yet in the coming out and going back its form is never seen. This is called the Heavenly Gate. The Heavenly Gate is non-being. The myriad things come forth from non-being. Being cannot create being out of being; inevitably it must come forth from non-being. Non-being is absolute non-being, and it is here that the sage hides himself' (Watson, 1968: 256–7). The term Heavenly Gate (*tian men*) means something similar to the version 'doorway to all subtleties' in Section 1 (DDJ). The 'sage' mentioned in this context appears somewhat as a god-like being. Furthermore, the English rendering of *You* as 'being' should be 'Being-within-form,' and that of *Wu* as 'non-being' should be 'Being-without-form.' For Zhuangzi's consideration of the two categories resumes Laozi's line of thought.

Incidentally, it has been argued for centuries that the concept of Being-without-form (*Wu*) be replaced by the concept of having-no-name (*wu ming*) or vice versa. It is the same case with the concept of Being-within-form (*You*) and that of having-name (*you ming*). This issue is in fact stemmed from the absence of punctuation in classical Chinese writings that are read and interpreted by means of sense group. Very often than not it gives rise to ambiguity when a sentence could be treated in two possible ways. Following Heshang Gong's and Wang Bi's steps, some modern Laozi scholars like Liu Xiaogan and others maintain that the concepts of having-no-name and having-name are more justifiable than those of Being-without-form and Being-within-form. For in Section 1 (DDJ) the Chinese words '*wu*' (having-no) and '*you*' (having) are used as adjectives for such abstract nouns as '*ming*' (name), and '*yu*' (desire). Thus they form such key concepts as '*wu ming*' (having-no-name), '*wu yu*' (having-no-desire) versus '*you ming*' (having-name) and '*you yu*' (having-desire). Accordingly, having-no-name indicates the fact of unnamability because of the chaotic state of the cosmos and the inadequate cognitive power of the primitives; and having-name implies the fact of namability due to the emergence of things and the adequate cognitive power of ancients then. This being the case, 'both having-no-name and having-name bear the fundamental properties of the universe. Although appearing to be different concepts, they are used to signify something similar, and hence "These two have the same source but different names" (*yi ming tong wei*). They seem to be opposite but interconnected, being knowable and unknowable in the mean time. Thus they both may be "the deepest and most profound" and consequently "the doorway to all subtleties"' (Liu, 2006: 98–100).

To mention in passing, some scholars tend to employ such terms as 'Non-being' for the Daoist concept of *Wu* and 'Being' for that of *You*. Yet, it is imperative to point out that this 'Non-being' in Laozi's thought does not mean 'nothing.' It is something real both in existence and in effect. It reflects the invisible or hidden character of the *Dao* as a kind of potentiality beyond our sensory perception. We assume that the concept of Being-without-form (*Wu*) is used by Laozi to describe the state of the *Dao* before it achieves its actuality or manifestation of Being-within-form (*You*). It is also worth stressing that the Daoist concept of 'Being' (*You*) is different in meaning from the 'Being' (*to on*) as expounded and articulated by Parmenides and Plato. This is just because the former, as the manifestation of the *Dao*, can be concrete and many, whereas the latter, owing to its transcendental trait, remains abstract and one. In short, the former is identified with the many of a material kind while the latter with the One of an immaterial kind.

In addition, the Chinese notion *xuan* is rendered here as 'deep and profound'. Wing-tsit Chan translates it as either 'profound' or 'mysterious.' He holds that the word itself has a wide range of meanings, as have many other Chinese words. It means dark, abstruse, deep, profound, secret, mysterious, and so forth. In Daoism as religion (*Dao jiao*), the aspect of mystery should be stressed; but in Daoism as philosophy (*Dao jiao*), the profound or metaphysical aspect is paramount. Thus *xuan xue* should be translated as 'metaphysical school,' while *xuan de* should be translated as 'profound and secret virtue.' These expressions simply have to be understood in their contexts involved. *Xuan ming*, for example, means not only 'profoundly dark,' but also noumenon in itself (Chan, 1973: 788).

Finally, 'the doorway to all subtleties' in the last line refers to the *Dao* as an all-embracing principle of the myriad things and their endless changes. Since the *Dao* is the unity of Being-without-form and Being-within-form, it operates at a deeper and more profound level, creating Heaven and Earth, generating, and transforming all under Heaven.

1.2 (Section 4)

The *Dao* is empty (like a bowl),
   Its usefulness can never be exhausted?
The *Dao* is bottomless (like a valley),
   And is perhaps the ancestor of all things.
Invisible or formless, it appears non-existing
   But actually it exists.
I don't know whose child it is at all?
It seems to have even preceded the Lord.

Commentary

The *Dao* is depicted in this section as being empty. The state of being empty and formless reflects the quality and substance of the *Dao*. However, this does not mean there is nothing in it at all. It actually embodies a dynamic potentiality and creative agency, which produces and functions inexhaustibly.

Though being empty and formless, the *Dao* is seen in Laozi's mind's eye to be far more essential and fundamental than the Lord of Heaven that had previously been respected as the ancestor of all things in the universe. Accordingly, the *Dao*, instead of the Lord, remains the origin of Heaven and Earth and the mother of all things.

It is interesting to notice that in Christianity the Lord has been all along worshiped as the creator of all beings. This was also true of the natural religion of ancient China. The ancients were then convinced that everything was invented and controlled by some supernatural power, because that they were unable to understand the natural elements and phenomena confronted. Their acquired knowledge of the external world was at a very low level. Hence they tended to ascribe whatever happened beyond their understanding to the divine power of supernatural beings they imagined to exist. There emerged therefore such notions as Lord (*di*), deity (*shen*), and spirits (*gui*). As time went by, people became skeptical about those notions, and in the era preceding Laozi's, the philosopher Zi Chan once remarked that 'The *Dao* of Heaven is remote while the *Dao* of human is close by.' This implicitly denies the fancied existence of the Heavenly Lord, and recommends a kind of not-to-bother attitude toward it. Meanwhile it reminds us of what Confucius said later about spirits and divine beings in a widely-quoted statement as follows: 'We should respect but keep aloof from the spirits and divine beings.' .

Notwithstanding that, there is no explicit denial of the existence of the Lord in such Chinese classics as *The Book of Poetry* (*Shi jing*), *The Book of Zuo Zhuan* (*Zuo zhuan*), and *The Conversations of the States* (*Guo yü*). In fact, nobody dared then to underestimate the supreme position of the Lord, despite a few complaints about injustice in the aspects of reward and punishment which were believed to be blindly exercised by the Lord. It was rather paradoxical that they would curse the Lord in view of the injustice they encountered, while still confessing to Him when wronged or ill-treated or harried into natural disasters. In striking contrast, Laozi's conception of the *Dao* instead of the Lord turns out to be overarching, and working as the ancestor of all things, as is confirmed in his conclusion that 'The *Dao* seems to have existed before the Lord' (*xiang di zhi xian*).

1.3 (Section 6)

The spirit of the valley is immortal.
   It is called the subtle and profound female.
The gate of the subtle and profound female
   Is the root of Heaven and Earth.
It is continuous and everlasting,
   With a utility never exhausted.

Commentary

This section again describes the magical productivity of the *Dao*. The term 'spirit' is used in a casual manner. It should be kept in mind that 'the spirit of the valley' (*gu shen*) has, as it were, nothing to do with any form of spiritual or divine beings in the above context. It factually refers to the wonderful *Dao* that features vacuity or emptiness, subtlety and constancy.

However, the expression 'the spirit of the valley' itself is rather ambiguous. Some Laozi scholars assume that 'valley' (*gu*) signifies a state of emptiness or virtuousness, and 'spirit' (*shen*) endless and unpredictable changes (e.g. Chen, 1992: 85–6). Some others think that 'the spirit of the valley' refers to an immortal deity in an empty or virtuous state (e.g. Ai, 1993: 27). I personally agree with the argument that the expression as such implies another name for the *Dao* itself (Sha, 1992: 10).

Noticeably, the metaphor 'subtle and profound female' (*xuan pin*) is largely derived from the worship of the female organ for its productiveness and mysteriousness in antiquity. It is here used for the *Dao*, symbolizing its invisible power or potentiality that produces all things. The expression that 'The gate of the subtle and profound female is the root of Heaven and Earth' is obviously identical in meaning to that 'Being-without-form is the beginning of Heaven and Earth,' and 'Being-within-form is the mother of all things.'

1.4 (Section 25)

There was something undifferentiated and all-embracing
    That existed before Heaven and Earth.
Soundless and formless as it is,
    It depends on nothing external and stays inexhaustible.
It operates with a circular motion and remains inextinguishable.
It may be considered the mother of all under Heaven.
I do not know its name, and hence call it the *Dao* far-fetchedly.
If forced to give it another name, I shall call it the Great.
The Great is boundless and thus functioning everywhere.
It is functioning everywhere and thus becoming far-reaching.
It is becoming far-reaching and thus returning to the original point.
Therefore the *Dao* is great.
Heaven is great.
Earth is great.
And Man is also great.
There are four great things in the universe,
And Man is one of them.
Man follows the way of Earth.
Earth follows the way of Heaven.
Heaven follows the way of the *Dao*.
And the *Dao* follows the way of spontaneity.

Commentary

This section attempts to expound, first of all, the existence of the *Dao* with such qualities as independence, everlastingness, and absoluteness, among others. It is, in short, the master producer of all things, and the ultimate law to be followed. Secondly, it exposes such fundamental features of the *Dao* as soundlessness, formlessness, greatness, and boundlessness. All this implies that the *Dao* embraces and affects all things, even though it is not directly observable or tangible. Thirdly, it illustrates the dynamic character of the *Dao* and its law of movement. The dialectic between its becoming its opposite and its returning to its original point is enlightening and instructive as regards the development and transition of world affairs in general, and social matters in particular. A detailed discussion will be supplied later when it comes to Section 40. Last but not least, it highlights the *Dao* as the way of spontaneity and as the ultimate law to be followed by Heaven, Earth, and man altogether. The *Dao* can be looked upon as the hidden measure or determinant of all under Heaven.

That 'It operates with a circular motion and remains inextinguishable' (*zhou xing*) leads to two chief interpretations: One claims that the *Dao* functions everywhere and permeates or internally determines everything (e.g. Heshang, 1991: 14; Wang, 1989: 6); the other assumes that *Dao* is always on the move, as though operating in a circular motion (e.g. Chen, 1992: 169). When taking into account the movement of the *Dao* (i.e. 'becoming far-reaching and thus returning to the original point,' and 'Reversion is the movement of *Dao*' (DDJ, Sect. 40), we are inclined to agree with the second explanation.

Ostensibly, Laozi is preoccupied with the idea that the *Dao* is creative, productive and the originator of the cosmos. His preferred employment of 'mother' (*mu*) as a metaphor for the *Dao* well confirms his stress on the feminine or *Yin* aspect of Chinese culture in general. He himself could hardly think of any available term for what he was pondering in his mind. However, he intended to introduce a new concept of his own in order to break down the theistic conventionalism characterized by the imagined pre-existence of the Lord *qua* the creator of all beings. Hence he offered a series of tentative alternatives apart from further relevant descriptions.

It is proclaimed in the *Yi zhuan* (Commentary on *The Book of Changes*) that there are three great things in the universe, namely, Heaven, Earth and man. Yet there is one more category according to Laozi, that is, the *Dao*, which is considered to be the origin of all. It is historically significant to rank man as one of the four great things in the universe. By so doing, man is placed in a position to make a proper use of the other three and even all things. As a matter of fact, the values of all other things would be reduced to nil if not for the existence of man. This naturally endows man with a supreme role that could be potentially positive and negative in consequence. It could be positive in that man remains rational and takes right actions. It could be negative in that man becomes emotional and takes wrong actions. It is for this reason that the moralization of man is always most important of all in the Chinese thought. Take the morality-based Confucianism for example. It attempts to transform humans into moral beings and expect them to exercise such values of universal love or reciprocal humanity in a secular world. Otherwise they might go to astray owing to their non-divine cultural heritage by nature. In contrast, Daoism places more emphasis on the nourishment of spiritual tranquility and advises people to embrace the idea of doing nothing against the *Dao* or taking no blind or wrong action.

Some Laozi scholars have misinterpreted the original expression of *dao fa zi ran* as 'The *Dao* follows nature.' The *Dao* is essentially natural and originally the mother of Heaven and Earth as another name for nature. When observing the working and essence of the *Dao* as a whole throughout this book, we tend to conclude that *zi ran* signifies 'spontaneity' or 'naturalness' in the context concerned. We therefore have rendered it thus: 'The *Dao* follows the way of spontaneity' (or the way of naturalness). 'The way of spontaneity' refers to the *Dao* itself in function.

Chapter 2

The Features of the Dao

Laozi's concept of the *Dao* serves as the keystone for his philosophy, and the starting point for his doctrine of the origin of the universe in particular. With high awareness of the duality of the *Dao*, known as Being-without-form and Being-within-form, Laozi exposes such general features as imagelessness, soundlessness, formlessness, vagueness and elusiveness of the *Dao* with regard to 'the inseparable One' (i.e. the *Dao*) and their interactions with their counterparts. In this section we concentrate on Sections 14, 35, 21, and 5 (DDJ).

2.1 (Section 14)

You look at it but cannot see it;
  It is called the imageless.
You listen to it but cannot hear it;
  It is called the soundless.
You touch it but cannot find it;
  It is called the formless.
These three cannot be further inquired into
  For they are the inseparable One.
The One is not bright when it is up,
  And not dark when it is down.
Infinite and indistinct, it cannot be named,
  Thus reverting to a state of non-thingness.

This is called shape without shape,
  Or image without image.
It is also called the Vague and the Elusive.
When meeting it, you cannot see its head.
When following it, you cannot see its back.
Hold on to the *Dao* of old,
  In order to harness present things.

From this you may know the primeval beginning.
This is called the law of the *Dao*.

Commentary

As stated in this section, the general features of the *Dao* appear to be multi-dimensional. They can be generalized as imagelessness, soundlessness, formlessness, shapelessness, vagueness, elusiveness and namelessness. They are also described as invisibility, intangibility, indescribability, and infinity. Yet, by scrutinizing them we may tentatively conclude that the *Dao* as such is characterized by these two fundamental aspects: first, 'it is not bright when it is up;' that is to say, the *Dao* is invisible and indistinct when it is above form. It simply transcends the empirical and corporeal things as well as physical perception. Secondly, 'it is not dark when it is down.' This means that the *Dao* becomes clear and manifest when it is within form, or, in other words, when it is transformed into the *De*. These two aspects could be likened to the metaphysical and physical dimensions.

The greatness or infinite nature of the *Dao* is revealed in the passage, 'When meeting it, you cannot see its head; when following it, you cannot see its back.' This is somewhat mystic at the first sight. But with regard to its non-observable aspect, the *Dao* itself seems to be omnipotent in effect.

The significance of the expression 'the *Dao* of old' lies in its efficacy in 'harnessing present things.' This indicates that the *Dao* in the abstract stays potentially in power for ever. When followed by humans, it helps them to tackle social issues, and govern a state or even the whole world in the most effective and peaceful manner. That is why Laozi strongly recommends people to 'hold on to it.' It is worth mentioning that such characteristics of the *Dao* (or the inseparable One) described as 'the Vague and Elusive' (*hu huang*) happen to be rather perplexing, because they are so nebulous. Nevertheless, those who are familiar with Chinese *qigong* would be most apt to understand the wording employed by Laozi. Chinese *qigong* is known as a system of deep breathing exercise with the purpose of spiritual nourishment and personal cultivation. It has been practiced in China since ancient times. Similar to meditation, it attempts to purify the mind and free it from inner tensions and desires, and even external temptations. Laozi advocates getting rid of selfishness and desires in order to return to the primeval state of simplicity and tranquility. Thus, I assume the practical approach to be associated with *qigong*.

The *Dao* is not manifest or visible when it is without form; it becomes clear and perceivable when it is within form as a result of its transformation into the *De*. These two aspects of the *Dao*, like the two sides of one model, turn out to be identical to Being-without-form and Being-within-form, as discussed previously with regard to the nature of the *Dao* (see 1.1). Moreover, 'the Vague and Elusive' aspects are compatible with the indescribable and unnamable features of the *Dao* (see 2.3).

2.2 (Section 35)

If you hold fast to the great image,
　　All the people under Heaven will come to you.
They will come and do no harm to each other,
　　But will all enjoy comfort, peace and health.
Music and dainties can make passers-by tarry,
　　While the *Dao*, if spoken out, is insipid and tasteless.
Being looked at, it is imperceptible.
Being listened to, it is inaudible.
Being utilized, it is inexhaustible.

Commentary

This section intends to exemplify the engaging power of the *Dao* in a social sense. A wise ruler who grasps the *Dao* is likely to win the hearts of all the people under Heaven; he will be then in a position to bring peace and order to the whole world, and accordingly make people feel secure, protected and happy. Unlike tangible and attractive things, for instance, 'music and dainties' or 'humanity and the rites' as fine-sounding promises, the *Dao* is insipid and tasteless, imperceptible and inaudible as well as inexhaustible. Nevertheless, it is capable of making the world peaceful and the people contented.

2.3 (Section 21)

The character of the great *Dao*
　　Follows from the *Dao* alone.
What is called the *Dao*
　　Appears elusive and vague.
Vague and elusive as it is,
　　There is the image in it.
Elusive and vague as it is,
　　There is the real in it.
Profound and obscure as it is,
　　There is the essence in it.
The essence is very concrete
　　And contains the proof inside itself.
From the present back to the past
　　Its name continues to ever last,
　　By which alone we may know the beginning of all things.
How do I know their beginning as such?
Only through this.

Commentary

Revealed in this section are the basic characteristics of the *Dao* that are incorporeal and invisible, but exist and function in reality. As can be noticed, 'the real' may be traced back to 'the image'; 'the image' may be traced back to 'the essence'; and 'the essence' can then be traced back to the *Dao* as a state of being 'vague and elusive.'

It is noteworthy that the historical development of Chinese art theory finds a permanent and permeable influence originating in the following statements: 'Elusive and vague as it is, there is the image in it. Vague and elusive as it is, there is the real in it. Profound and obscure as it is, there is the essence in it.' The *Dao* of Chinese art is said to lie in the ideal and achievement of the poetic state par excellence (*yi jing*), which is largely determined by image beyond form (*xiang wai zhi xiang*) and significance beyond charm (*yun wai zhi zhi*), and so forth. Take Chinese landscape painting (freehand brushwork painting in particular) for example: It always places the stress on the realization of the poetic state *par excellence* (*yi jing*) and of the inner spirit-likeness (*shen si*). Thus a Chinese artist tends to care less than his occidental counterpart for perspective as a technique to produce three-dimensionality and life likeness via elaborate imitation. Rather, he pays more attention to creating a vivid touch to convey the inner spirit, say, using the form outward to show the spirit inward. That is why Chinese freehand brush-work painting is often characterized by spontaneous expression and bold outline instead of an authentically identifiable object. It would be relevant and instructive to examine the following reference in Section 14: 'It is called shape without shape or image without object. It is also called a state of being vague and elusive.'

In addition, the original term *kong de* is translated into 'the great *De*' and is regarded as the manifestation of the *Dao*. Its quality is all-embracing, operating in everything and everywhere. The *De* works in conformity with the *Dao* simply because the former is the manifestation of the latter. Since they are interrelated, one must bear in mind the fact that the *Dao* is something like an omniprinciple underlying all things, whereas the *De* exhibits the power of the *Dao* through observable functions.

2.4 (Section 5)

Heaven and Earth are not humane.
They regard all things as straw dogs.
The sage is not humane?
He regards all people as straw dogs.
The space between Heaven and Earth is like a bellows, isn't it?
While vacuous, it is never exhaustible.

When active, it turns out even more.
(To talk too much will surely lead to a quick demise.
   Hence, it is better to keep to tranquility.)

Commentary

This section seems to focus on the inhumanity (*bu ren*) of Heaven, Earth and the Doaist sage as well. By reading between the lines, one could discover that Laozi's philosophy of take-no-action is part and parcel of his whole exposition. The inhumanity of this kind can well be seen as an extension of his principal idea of take-no-action. Heaven and Earth follow the way of naturalness without taking arbitrary action. Yet, they incessantly generate one thing after another. Similarly, the sage conforms to the way of naturalness without taking blind action, yet he enables people to maintain their genuine selves and become what they should be. The opposite of 'take-no-action' is 'take-action' of which 'too much talk' is a concrete example in bad governance. Then what would happen in the end if 'take-action' of this type were put into practice? It would be nothing but a quickened failure. Therefore Laozi reckons that 'It is better to keep to tranquility.'

   Similarly, Zhuangzi regards 'supreme humanity' (*zhi ren*) as 'inhumanity' (*bu ren*) from a peculiar viewpoint. He holds that Heaven and Earth that possess Great Beauty remain silent. Heaven and Earth have Great Humanity but never show it off. As a consequence of following the way of Heaven and Earth, the Daoist sage, in his conduct of war, might destroy a country without losing the hearts of the people. His benefits might extend to ten thousand generations without being a lover of man. Why is it so? Because Zhuangzi maintains that he who purposely manifests affection is not a man of humanity. Likewise, the Daoist sage is not humane even though his blessing reaches all generations; he is not old even though he is more ancient than the highest antiquity; and he is not skillful even though he covers Heaven, supports Earth and fashions the various forms of all things.

   As for the simile 'bellows' (*tuo yue*) used by Laozi for the space between Heaven and Earth, it can be viewed as a symbol of the *Dao* in terms of its characteristics like emptiness and inexhaustibility. As regards the metaphor 'the store of nature' (*tian fu*) employed by Zhuangzi, it suggests the potentiality of the *Dao*. The store is not full when things are put in it; it is not empty when things are taken out of it. Its function of this kind easily reminds us of 'the spirit of the valley' in Laozi's terminology. The valley is deep and bottomless, serving as the source of all things. What is inside can never be used up merely because it is able to accommodate and generate so many things.

   It must be pointed out that Heaven and Earth appear as physical and natural entities. They follow the way of spontaneity inasmuch as they have no preference for anything in the world. They let all things be what they are or let them go through a natural cycle, for instance, the change and replacement of the four seasons, the life and death of human beings, the appearance and disappearance of plants, the shift of day and night, so on and so forth. By this statement Laozi attempts to explain the fact that Heaven and Earth have no feelings and emotions directed toward particular beings. They simply treat all things equal and alike.

Incidentally, the 'straw dogs' (*chu gou*) refers to part of the sacrificial offerings for worshiping Heaven. After the ceremonies they would be discarded as worthless. They are used here as a metaphor, suggesting that Heaven and Earth show no sympathy for anything or anybody. They stick to the way of naturalness. This is relevant to Laozi's conception that 'Man follows the way of Earth; Earth follows the way of Heaven; Heaven follows the way of the *Dao*; and the *Dao* follows the way of spontaneity.'

Talking about the universe, Laozi exhibits his individual insight and striking imagination. As a result, he likens the vast space between Heaven and Earth to a bellows featuring emptiness, productiveness and inexhaustibility. The image itself is fresh and unique, exemplifying the style of Laozi as a philosophical poet.

By 'To talk too much' (*duo yan*) is meant too many political orders, monarchical decrees, secular moral lessons, and so forth. If a government issues too many orders, it will surely find itself running counter to its goals and speed up its demise. As a matter of fact, an efficient government does not have to do so. Historically, it has been proved that the more the official orders that emanate from the government, the less effective they are and the swifter the decline of the prestige of the government. Such a situation leads to a government that only has the ability to issue political orders, and lacks the ability to carry them out.

Contained in many DDJ editions is the expression *bu ru shou zhong*, which is translated into English as 'holding on to the mean' (Henricks), or as 'It is better to keep to the center' (Chan). These renditions are rather misleading because they tend to make the reader conceive this notion from the Confucian doctrine of the golden mean (*zhong yong*). Some Laozi scholars such as Yan Lingfeng and Chen Guying (1992: 82) assume that the Chinese word *zhong* (center or the mean) may be a printing error or misspelling of *chong* (empty or vacuous). Hence it is translated into English as 'Better to hold fast to the void' (Lau). Other scholars tend to agree that the term *zhong* (center) might stand for the center of a bellows, which is empty or void inside. In addition, scholars like Ma Xulun and Gao Heng (1988: 15) proclaim that the last two lines ('To talk too much will surely lead to a quick demise. Hence it is better to keep to tranquility.') do not suit the context at all. That is why Gu Ji and Zhou Ying (1991: 640) inserts them in the original Section 9 (DDJ). No matter which is the case, the concept of *zhong* is reckoned to be associated with such features as emptiness and inexhaustibility, having nothing to do with the doctrine of the mean in Confucianism.

Chapter 3

The Movement of the Dao

The motion of the *Dao* is considered to have a dialectical character that reflects the growth, change, and decline of all things in a developmental cycle. The idea associated with 'reversion' (*fan*), if not absolutized as it is by Laozi, can still have a valid message even judged from a modern perspective. Let us look into Section 40 (DDJ).

3.1 (Section 40)

Reversion is the movement of the *Dao*.
Weakness is the function of the *Dao*.
All things under Heaven come from Being-within-form
And Being-within-form comes from Being-without-form.

Commentary

Brief and concise as it is, this section is strikingly rich in connotations. It is generally concluded that Laozi exposes his dialectical concept of the *Dao* in terms of its movement and function, which in turn comes to be a law of change and transformation from one side to its opposite. According to the observations by some Laozi scholars, 'reversion' (*fan*) refers to a kind of interrelation between opposites in one sense, and in another sense, a kind of return to the root known as the unity of opposites (Chen, 1992: 223–4). We think that the movement of the *Dao* in such a manner of 'reversion' may be well symbolized by the *tai ji*, in which the two forces known as *Yin* and *Yang* are always in motion, interdependent and interacting at the same time. The generalization that 'reversion is the movement of the *Dao*' can be seen as a refined version of what is said about the *Dao* in Section 25. It is noticeable throughout human history that things (i.e. a nation, culture, economic strength, political power, etc.) are doomed to roll downhill once they reach their acme. This indicates that they tend to reverse to their opposites in an ever-changing process. If we give due consideration to our surroundings, for example, the changes detected in plants and the stages experienced in the life cycle, we may collect sufficient evidence to justify the dialectical movement of the *Dao*. It is schematically interesting to quote a well-known Chinese saying as follows: 'Things that are too high fall down easily; things that are too white stain easily; songs that are too pretentious have few listeners; reputations that are too lofty often fall short of reality' (Kiu, 1991: 129). All these possibilities seem to be in conformity with the Chinese conception of 'Inevitable reversal of the extreme' (*wu ji bi fan*).

It is worth mentioning that Laozi, even though emphasizing the opposing interrelationship between things and the significant role of their transaction or transformation, ultimately focuses on the idea of returning to the root as the final destination for all things. For it is right there in his idea that absolute stillness, tranquility or state of take-no-action will be actualized, and accordingly all the conflicts and antitheses in the world will draw to an end.

The statement, 'Weakness is the function of the *Dao*' is in fact a further justification of the foregoing assertion that 'Reversion is the movement of the *Dao*.' Laozi's philosophy features a preference for 'cleaving to the soft and weak' (*shou ruo*). He often uses water (*shui*) as an image to illustrate the overwhelming power of 'the soft and weak.' It is helpful for a better understanding of this notion if we approach it with reference to his discussion in Section 78. That is, 'Nothing under Heaven is softer and weaker than water, and yet nothing can compare with it in attacking the hard and strong . . . (*tian xia zhi ruo mo guo yu shui, er gong jian qiang zhe mo zhi neng xian . . .*).' However, one should be aware of the problematic aspect of Laozi's confirmation that the soft and the weak are bound to conquer the hard and the strong. This is largely due to his absolutization of the former by cutting it off from actual and varying conditions in both subjective and objective domains.

Also offered in this section is a generalized explication of how all things under the sky come into being. It is here once again that Laozi traces the origin of the universe. Both Being-within-form and Being-without-form are different names for the *Dao*, and are likened to the two sides of the same coin. In short, the expression in this context is a modified as well as a condensed one of the ideas presented in Section 1 (see 1.1).

Once again the two notions of 'reversion' (*fan*) and 'weakness' (*ruo*) are rather crucial and decisive. The former contains a similar meaning in this context as it does in Section 25 'The Great is boundless and thus functioning everywhere. It is functioning everywhere and thus becoming far-reaching. It is becoming far-reaching and thus returning to the original point.' In addition, it is used here to signify a dynamic and circular movement of the *Dao*. The latter is ambiguous. There are so far a number of interpretations of this, of which we cite three key ones as follows: first, it is supposed to denote the function of the *Dao* that exemplifies itself through the soft and weak; secondly, the function of the *Dao* lies in helping all things grow and become complete naturally without any imposing force; and finally, the function of the

Dao displays itself by the dialectical fact that the soft and the weak are to overcome the hard and the strong (*rou rou sheng gang qiang*) as is so hypothesized by Laozi. I personally am inclined to agree with the third interpretation since it corresponds in principle to Laozi's proposal on 'keeping to the soft and the weak' (*shou rou*).

Chapter 4

The Dao *and the Myriad Things*

Laozi holds the view that the *Dao* is the omniprinciple of all individual principles. Thus the *Dao* produces all things, and all things then develop from the *Dao*. The interactions and interrelations between the *Dao* and all things are in fact the extension of his theory about the ultimate origin of the universe. This thought-way can still find its traces and influences deeply-set in the mentality of the Chinese people today. To be chiefly discussed in this part are the Sections 42, 32, 34, and 39 (DDJ).

4.1 (Section 42)

The *Dao* produces the One.
The One turns into the Two.
The Two give rise to the Three
The Three bring forth the myriad of things.
The myriad things contain *Yin* and *Yang* as vital forces,
Which achieve harmony through their interactions.

Commentary

This section discusses the originality of the *Dao* and the emergence of the universe. The concepts of 'the One,' 'the Two,' and 'the Three' are symbolically employed to explicate the process of how the *Dao* produces the myriad things. This process is characterized with an evolution from the simple to the complex, which happens to reflect the development of all creation.

As is described specifically in this section, 'the One' stands for the Whole as the Ultimate Origin of Heaven and Earth. It is allegorically perceived as the chaos of the universe where everything stayed in an original state of entirety or without discrimination in between. It can be said to be another name for the *Dao* as the beginning of all things. In Chinese language 'the One' also features absolute uniqueness and unity as well.

'The Two' refer to two vital forces known as *Yin* and *Yang*. A further rendering of *Yin* and *Yang* may be as two essential kinds of *qi* (vital energy or life force) that oppose and complement each other. The ancient Chinese people in general and thinkers in particular believed that all things were produced as a result of the complementary interaction between *Yin* and *Yang*.

'The Three' could be interpreted as three types of vital energy owing to the interaction of *Yin* and *Yang*: The first type may be *yin sheng zhi qi* meaning that the *Yin* vital energy (*yin qi*) overwhelms the *Yang* vital energy (*yang qi*); the second type may be *yang sheng zhi qi* meaning that the *Yang* vital energy overwhelms the *Yin* vital energy; and the third type may be *chongqi* meaning that the synthesis of the *Yin* vital energy and its *Yang* counterpart will be forming into a harmonious realm. However, Fung Yu-lan assumes that *chong qi* is another kind of vital energy encompassing the *Yin* vital energy and the *Yang* vital energy within itself, and therefore similar to 'the One' or the *Dao* in this context (Fung, 1992: 50).

4.2 (Section 32)

The *Dao* is eternal and has no name.
Though it is simple and seems minute,
    Nothing under Heaven can subordinate it.
If kings and lords were able to maintain it,
    All people would submit to them spontaneously.
Heaven and Earth unite to drip sweet dew,
    Without the command of men, it drips evenly over all.
Once a system comes into being,
    Names are instituted.
Once names are instituted,
    One has to know where and when to stop.
It is by knowing where and when to stop
    That one can be free from danger.
Everything under Heaven is embraced by the *Dao*,
    Just like every river or stream running into the sea.

Commentary

Laozi makes simplicity a virtue of the *Dao*, which in turn reflects the primitiveness of the *Dao*. This notion in fact signifies the way of spontaneity (i.e. naturalness) and take-no-action. If a leader can hold on to it and put it into practice, he is sure to win the people over and govern the country in peace.

The great (*da*) and the minute (*xiao*) are obviously antithetic in common sense, but implicitly interrelated in the functioning of the *Dao*, somewhat similar to

Being-within-form and Being-without-form as two complementary aspects. Both the great and the minute are abstract terms. The former suggests that the *Dao* embraces and covers all in that 'when meeting it, you cannot see its head; while following it, you cannot see its back.' The latter implies that the *Dao* is invisible and formless to the extent that it permeates and determines everything everywhere.

The 'sweet dew' as a product of the *Dao* 'drips evenly over all.' This demonstrates that the *Dao* treats all things alike, as though it embodies a spirit of equality. Modest and accommodating, the *Dao* receives all things in the way the sea receives every river and stream. Hence it becomes boundless and inexhaustible. Even so, it does not claim any glory for itself but lets things be what they are. The parabolic depiction of the *Dao* through the image of the sea also carries the message that the *Dao* renews itself due to its receptiveness. It is something that remains open to all for ever. This is compatibly true of Laozi's philosophical system that always provokes new thoughts whenever it is read and reread.

As mentioned in this section, Laozi reminds people of the importance of knowing where and when to stop once names of ranking positions, for example, were introduced. This in fact advises people to bridle their desires and to be contented with what they have. Otherwise they may get into trouble in the course of their hot and blind pursuit of external temptations.

4.3 (Section 34)

The great *Dao* flows everywhere.
It may go left, it may go right.
All things rely on it for existence,
　　And never does it turn away from them.
When it accomplishes its work,
　　It does not claim credit for itself.
It preserves and nourishes all things,
　　But it does not claim to be master over them.
Thus it may be called the minute.
All things come to it as to their home,
　　Yet it does not act as their master.
Hence it may be called the great.
This is always the case with the sage
　　Who is able to achieve his greatness
　　Just because he himself never strives to be great.

Commentary

This section shows the function of the *Dao* related to the development of all things. The function as such lies in 'following spontaneity' and features a kind of selflessness. According to Laozi, the *Dao* is the mother or creator of all things in the world. However, what it does is to help them grow and become what they are, never claiming the accomplishments for its own and never attempting to dominate anything at all. Therefore the *Dao* appears as a generous giver or nurturer in respect of all its surroundings.

The sage lauded above is always the Daoist type. He follows the *Dao* as the ultimate example and approaches it through his action upon it. The reason why he is 'able to achieve his greatness' can be multi-fold. Since 'he never strives himself to be great,' he makes no distinction between 'the great' (*da*) and 'the minute' (*xiao*) that are part of the nature of the *Dao*. Since he makes no distinction between them, he acts without any preference or calculation in favor of this or that. This approach is in the long run positive in the accumulation of achievements on the one hand, and on the other, it serves to free him from being a 'tall poppy' that is prone to be cut down in a competitive world.

4.4 (Section 39)

Of those in the past that obtained the One
Heaven obtained the One and became clear;
The Earth obtained the One and became tranquil;
The Gods obtained the One and became divine;
The Valleys obtained the One and became full;
All things obtained the One, and became alive and kept growing;
Kings and lords obtained the One and the world became peaceful.

Taking this to its logical conclusion we may say:
If Heaven had not thus become clear,
   It would soon have cracked;
If the Earth had not thus become tranquil,
   It would soon have broken apart;
If the Gods had not thus become divine,
   They would soon have perished;
If the valleys had not thus become full,
   They would soon have dried up;
If all things had not thus become alive and kept growing,
   They would soon have become extinct;
If kings and lords had not thus become honorable and noble,
   They would soon have toppled and fallen.

It is always the case
   That the noble takes the humble as its root
   And the high takes the low as its base.
Hence kings and lords call themselves

The orphaned, the solitary or the unworthy.
This is regarding the humble as the root of the noble.
   Is it not?
People disdain the 'orphaned,' 'solitary' or 'unworthy.'
And yet kings and lords call themselves by these terms.
Therefore the highest honor needs no flattering.
Thus with everything –
   Sometimes it may increase when decreased,
   And sometimes it may decrease when increased.
For this reason –
   They desire not to dazzle and glitter like jade,
   But to remain firm and plain like stone.

Commentary

In this section one may well observe that gods even became divine with the help of the One as another term for the *Dao* in Laozi's discourse. It is also noticeable in the context that gods appear liable to meet the same fate as the others that fail to attain the One (i.e. the *Dao*). In addition, gods are ranked (possibly in chronological order) after Heaven and Earth. This may indicate that Heaven and Earth precede gods in Laozi's perspective (see Section 4 for an identical case in which the Lord or God is filed after the *Dao*). Nevertheless, they are all in the same boat by virtue of the fact that they are likely to vanish if unable to grasp the *Dao*. In plain language, no matter what they may be (e.g. Heaven, Earth, gods, valleys, the myriad things, kings, marquises, etc.), they are doomed to failure or extinction if they betray or deviate from the *Dao*. This is precisely because the *Dao* in Laozi's mind serves as the source of all energies and the origin of all things. It does not merely generate everything, but determines everything. It seems to work as a frame of reference for all. In comparing the *Dao* with gods, the former stays primary and original, whereas the latter secondary and derivative.

The capitalized 'One' here is equivalent to the Chinese concept of *yi*. As can be detected in the Laozi book, this term usually carries a twofold sense as follows: first, it stands for the *Dao* as an omnipotent power that produces and underlies all things; secondly, it refers to the vital energy in chaos or the primitive matter coming from the *Dao*.

In respect to the relationship between the *Dao* and all things, as explicated by Laozi, his absolutization of the *Dao* turns out to be rather problematic and arbitrary. He dogmatically asserts that the destiny of all things lies in the palm of the *Dao* without any exception. This seems to be somewhat misleading because it leaves no room for the initiatives and variables in existence.

According to Ren Jiyu, this section begins with the universality and importance of the *Dao* from which Heaven, Earth, spirits, valleys, rulers, and the myriad things come. It goes on to argue that without the *Dao*, or going contrary to it, all things from Heaven and Earth to kings and princes will exist no more. Epithets such as the orphaned (*gu*), the solitary (*gua*), and the unworthy (*bu gu*) by which rulers used to refer to themselves in the olden days are by no means flattering terms, but through such derogatory names they could actually make their majesty and nobility obvious and salient. Laozi preaches that one should not be at the front, nor be the last, so that one can be free from danger (1993: 58).

Regarding kingship and lordship, Laozi claims that 'If kings and lords had not thus become honorable and noble, they would soon have toppled and fallen.' This is ostensibly a good-natured warning offered to rulers in general. According to Laozi, rulers are likely to be overthrown and discarded if they fail to conduct state affairs by means of reliable policies and a noble spirit. Or in modern terms, a government of whatever kind is apt to deteriorate if it happens to grow power-oriented instead of people-oriented.

One may find it somewhat peculiar when reading these two lines as follows: 'Sometimes it may increase when decreased, and sometimes it may decrease when increased.' Actually this idea demonstrates a dialectical speculation as regards decrease and increase. Subjectively speaking, when one is modest enough to lower himself as if decreasing his self-esteem, he is liable to be easily accepted by others and win their respect and thus enjoys a kind of increase of his self-esteem, and vice versa. Objectively speaking, things may well suffer from a decrease when they are meant to be increased; they are likely to have an increase when they are deliberately to be decreased. It seems that Laozi intends to encourage people in general and rulers in particular to be modest and humble in one sense, and expect things to develop in a natural way in another sense.

Interestingly, Laozi expects kings and lords to 'desire not to dazzle and glitter like jade, but to remain firm and plain like stone.' By this statement is meant that the sage ruler in Laozi's mind should remain modest, plain, and simple instead of being arrogant, self-important, or showy. Otherwise his self-image as well as authority will be subject to decrease rather than increase.

By the way, according to Heshang Gong's interpretation, a line in Section 39 (DDJ) is supposed to be '*hi shu ju wu ju*,' and according to Wang Bi's text, it is supposed to be '*zhi shu yu wu yu*.' In ancient Chinese language, '*ju*' and '*yu*' mean the same in this case, that is, car, chariot, or carriage. In the English translation by Arthur Waley, it is rendered into 'Enumerate the parts of a carriage, and you still have not explained what a carriage is' (1994: 91). In the English version by Wing-tsit Chan, it is rendered into 'Therefore enumerate all the parts of a chariot as you may, and you still have no chariot' (1973: 160). As is noticed in the findings made by some Laozi scholars like Fan Yingyuan, Wu Cheng, Gao Yandi, and Chen Guying, among others, the original sentence should be '*zhi yu wu yu*' (Chen, 1992: 221). Here the '*yu*' (honor) in old spelling appears somewhat similar to '*yu*' (chariot). Hence when copied onto another piece of bamboo slip, there would be a misspelling in this case. However, the word '*yu*' in the later findings means 'honor'. So the line '*zhi yu wu yu*' is translated into 'The highest honor needs no flattering' here in this volume. Some other versions put it into 'Supreme praise is no praise.' According to the context concerned, I think the altered translation based on the new findings makes much more sense. I hereby quote another translation for your reference only. That is, 'Therefore to seek too much honor means to lose honor wholly' (Ren, 1993: 59)

Chapter 5

The Dao *of Heaven and the* Dao *of Human*

The distinction between the *Dao* of Heaven and the *Dao* of human is set out in striking contrast. The former is symbolic of naturalness, selflessness, and equality in a virtuous sense. It is therefore recommended by Laozi. Yet, it is also viewed as a measurement for the latter that is confused with pretentiousness, selfishness, and inequality in a negative sense. Their respective services and differences are basically reflected in Sections 77 and 79 (DDJ).

5.1 (Section 77)

Does not the *Dao* of Heaven resemble the drawing of a bow?
When the string is taut, press it down.
When it is low, raise it up.
When it is excessive, reduce it.
When it is insufficient, supplement it.
The *Dao* of Heaven reduces whatever is excessive
   And supplements whatever is insufficient.
The *Dao* of human does the opposite.
It reduces the insufficient,
   And adds more to the excessive.
Who is able to have a surplus to offer to the world?
Only the one who has the *Dao*.
The sage does not accumulate for himself.
The more he shares with others, the more he possesses.
The more he gives to others, the richer he becomes.
The *Dao* of Heaven benefits all things and causes no harm.
The *Dao* of the sage acts for others but never competes with them.

Commentary

From his empirical observation of such natural phenomena as transition and change, motion and replacement, growth and decline, rise and fall, and life and death of all beings in the world, Laozi reaches the conclusion that there is such a thing as the *Dao* of Heaven, which, in its function as the law of nature, lets all things become what they can be without imposing, dominating, or taking any action. The *Dao* of Heaven is the heart of the universe that retains all things in balance.

Then, based on his observation of the reality in that chaotic and harsh age in which he lived, rent by repeated clashes and wars between the kingdoms, Laozi delineates the *Dao* of human as a general social law or code of human conduct similar to the 'law of the jungle.' He postulates rapacity and possessiveness as fundamental characteristics of the *Dao* of human.

According to Laozi's thought in its entirety, the *Dao* of human itself, if practiced and worshiped, will surely excite insatiable greed and desires for more possessions; this will inevitably lead to man-by-man exploitation, class discrimination, interpersonal struggles, and eventually social conflict and suffering. In a word, it is conducive to a vicious circle. That is why it must be condemned and abandoned.

In respect to the negative aspects of the *Dao* of human, Laozi recommends the *Dao* of Heaven not only as a counterbalance, but also as an ultimate criterion or frame of reference owing to its great virtues such as the universal heart of selflessness and the noble spirit of balancing all under Heaven. That is to say, the *Dao* of Heaven must be imitated, followed and acted upon by humans. This is merely Laozi's ideal as a result of his deep concern and sympathy for the tragic human condition in his era. Good-intentioned as it may be, this recommendation is after all wishful thinking in the presence of the harsh reality. But this does not necessarily mean that his wish and hope bear no message with regard to the keenly competitive and frustratingly problematic society in which we live nowadays.

It is worth mentioning in passing that the *Dao* of Heaven is also reflected in Laozi's remark that 'Heaven and Earth unite to drop sweet dew which falls evenly over all things without being forced.' All this could be seen as the source of the notion of egalitarianism or equal division of property which is deeply rooted in the mentality of the Chinese people. Hence, when its merit is appreciated for the sake of social stability, its demerits should not be neglected in terms of economic development. The Chinese nationals are fairly sensitive and highly conscious of the painstaking efforts made so far to break up the 'iron rice bowl' (i.e. 'equal pay for unequal work') in the course of China's current program of social and economic reform.

The sage is 'the only one who has the *Dao*' (i.e. the *Dao* of Heaven) and is characterized by such virtues as universal love and generosity. The *Dao* of the sage is the realization and extension of the *Dao* of Heaven in society or human praxis. All humans alike are encouraged not simply to heed the virtues of the Daoist sage, but also to act upon them in pursuit of personal development. Only by so doing, according to Laozi, people can live in harmony and society can be at peace.

When reading this section, one may find a couple of things noteworthy. First, by likening the *Dao* of Heaven to 'the drawing of a bow,' Laozi is trying to tell us allegorically how the *Dao* as such works. The process of drawing a bow involves aiming an arrow at a target, and naturally requires some form of corresponding adjustment. As is described subsequently in this section, this adjustment is spontaneously conducted by the *Dao* of Heaven which sets a model for humans to learn from and act upon. Secondly, the *Dao* of human, in contrast to the *Dao* of Heaven, 'reduces the insufficient, and adds more to the excessive.' The depiction here is intended to show how the *Dao* of human as a social law or code of human conduct functions and differs from the *Dao* of Heaven. This can be traced back to the historical background of the Spring and Autumn Period (722–481 BC) in ancient China, when conflicts and clashes were of frequent occurrence, actually stirred up by desires for more land, power and property. Therefore, Laozi reveals the *Dao* of human from a critical viewpoint. Thirdly, by claiming that 'The *Dao* of Heaven reduces whatever is excessive and supplements whatever is insufficient,' Laozi arrives at a conclusion from his intuitive as well as empirical observation of natural phenomena. In his eyes, such phenomena as the transition from day to night, the succession of the four seasons, the life and death of all beings appear to feature paradoxically antithesis and identity, in addition to equality and unity. Viewed from an immediate perspective, they all seem to be naturally or spontaneously what they are instead of being forced or dominated by an external power. Hence Laozi generalizes this situation as the *Dao* of Heaven for it corresponds to his philosophy of 'following the way of spontaneity' and 'take-no-action.' Finally, included in Section 81 in many Chinese versions of the DDJ are these lines as follows: 'The sage does not accumulate for himself. The more he shares with others, the more he possesses. The more he gives to others, the richer he becomes. The *Dao* of Heaven benefits all things and causes no harm. The *Dao* of the sage acts for others but never competes with them.' We rearrange them into this place according to a contextual analysis (Gu and Zhou, 1991: 594–604).

5.2 (Section 79)

To reconcile two sides in deep hatred
  Is surely to leave some hatred behind.
If one returns good for evil
  How can this be taken as a proper solution?
Therefore the sage keeps the counterfoil of the tally,
  Yet he does not demand payment of the debt.
The virtuous man is as kind and generous as the tally keeper
  While the non-virtuous is as harsh and calculating as a tax collector.
The *Dao* of Heaven has no preference.
It is constantly with the good man.

Commentary

That 'one should return good for evil' is well-noted as Laozi's idealized solution to hatred. It is offered to the people in general and the ruler in particular. In a totalitarian country the government tends to be power-oriented and property-hungry. Thus it is apt to apply policies of heavy taxation and severe punishments. This brings about an accumulation of complaints and growth of hatred which may some day explode as suddenly as a dormant volcano. The history of China is full of instances of revolts and rebellions caused by such policies.

The *Dao* of Heaven that 'has no preferences' is clearly personified by Laozi. It serves as a mirror of Daoist ideals in contrast to the *Dao* of human that goes around with preferences. The former is positive while the latter negative; likewise, he (e.g. a ruler) who practices the former is 'kind and generous' to the extent that he will be supported and beloved, whereas he (e.g. a ruler) who adopts the latter is 'harsh and calculating' to the extent that he will be cursed and overthrown. This moral lesson is still valid for leaders nowadays.

Chapter 6

From the Dao *into the* De

In Laozi's opinion, both the *Dao* and the *De* are in existence and effect. One is invisible while the other is visible. The interaction between the two can be likened to that between Being-without-form and Being-within-form. As a matter of fact, the *De* is seen as the manifestation of the *Dao*. The transformation from the *Dao* into the *De* is highly necessary, for the *Dao* would be otherwise a disembodied idea and possibly lose its existential rationale. The qualities of the *De* actually embody the potentiality or potency of the *Dao* itself.

Both the *Dao* and *De* have a variety of interpretations, such as the Way and its Power, the Way and its Potency, the all-embracing principle for all things and the individual principle underlying each thing, the omni-determinant of all beings and its manifestation, among others. No matter what they may be, there is an interaction between them and a transformation from one into the other. This topic is to be explored with particular reference to Sections 51 and 38 (DDJ).

6.1 (Section 51)

The *Dao* begets all beings,
  And the *De* fosters them.
Substance gives them physical forms,
  And the environment completes them.
Therefore all beings venerate the *Dao* and honor the *De*.
As for the veneration of the *Dao* and the honoring of the *De*,
  It is not out of obedience to any orders;
  It comes spontaneously due to their naturalness.
Hence the *Dao* begets all beings,
  And the *De* fosters them, rears them and develops them,
  Matures them and makes them bear fruit,
  Protects them and helps them breed.
To produce them without taking possession of them,
  To raise them without vaunting this as its own merit,

And to nourish them without controlling them,
This is called the Profound *De*.

Commentary

This section reconfirms Laozi's idea that the *Dao* begets all beings alike without
being observed since it works in the way of 'taking-no-action.' Then *De* as its
potency and manifestation fosters all beings through observable means such as
'substance,' 'environment,' 'sweet dew,' selfless protection, and so on. By
scrutinizing the text one can discern that the growth of all beings undergoes
such a process as generalized as follows: The *Dao* produces them all first, and
then it stays inherent in them and transforms itself into the *De* as the principle
of each individual being; in accordance with the *De* all beings develop with
individual characteristics; finally they grow mature or become what they are
with the help of their surroundings or environment (Chen, 1992: 246). During
this process as a whole, the *Dao* is venerated and the *De* honored for they both
follow the way of spontaneity or naturalness when begetting and fostering all
beings. In other words, they are free from any imposing action or force such
that they let things be what they can be, or become what they can become. They
themselves serve as natural laws allowing all things to develop without any
consciousness or purposefulness. Thus, they are characterized by great virtue in
giving birth and freedom, and offering help and protection selflessly to all
beings. In the end they do not claim any merit for what they have done, through
which the existence and development of all creation is rendered possible.

The 'Profound *De*' as the manifestation of the *Dao* can well be termed the
'Great Virtue' which transcends mundane values entangled with desires,
conflicts, competitions, gains and losses. 'The Profound *De*' can be looked
upon as a special part of the nature of the *Dao*, and a general spirit embodied
in Laozi's philosophizing. In addition, it is, explicitly or implicitly, advocated
to be adopted and conducted by mankind as a solution to the problems with
the human condition. If we review Laozi's thought in respect of the issues
which we confront nowadays, we may find it still instructive to a great extent.

It is worth pointing out that the term 'environment' is a translation of the
Chinese word *shi*, and connotes chiefly living, geographical, regional and
climatic conditions. It is also interpreted as the natural force derived from the
change of the seasons (Heshang, 1991:28), the potential power underlying
each individual thing, or the dynamic state lying in opposites like *Yin* and *Yang*
and their interaction in all beings (Chen, 1992:261–2).

Incidentally, the lines which start with 'To produce them without taking
possession of them . . .' were misplaced in Section 10 in some DDJ versions.
The original term *xuan de* is rendered as 'the Profound *De*' suggesting the
depth, profundity, selflessness, and transcendence of the *De* as such. It in fact
exhibits the function and potency of the *Dao*.

6.2 (Section 38)

The man of the superior *De* is not conscious of his *De*
   And in this way he really possesses the *De*.
The man of the inferior *De* never loses sight of his *De*
   And in this way he has no true *De*.
The man of the superior *De* takes no action
   And thus nothing will be left undone.
The man of the inferior *De* takes action
   And thus something will be left undone.
The man of superior humanity takes action
   And so acts without purpose.
The man of superior righteousness takes action
   And so acts on purpose.
The man of superior propriety takes action,
   And when people do not respond to it,
   He will stretch out his arms and force them to comply.

Therefore, only when the *Dao* is lost does the *De* disappear.
Only when the *De* is lost does humanity appear.
Only when humanity is lost does righteousness appear.
Only when righteousness is lost does propriety appear.

Now propriety is a superficial expression of loyalty and faithfulness,
   And the beginning of disorder.
The man of foreknowledge has but the flower of the *Dao*
   And this is the beginning of ignorance.
Hence the great man dwells in the thick instead of the thin.
He dwells in the fruit instead of the flower.
Therefore he rejects the latter and accepts the former.

Commentary

The word '*De*' generally means 'virtue' in both an ethical and social sense. It also denotes the realization and acquisition of the *Dao*. The cultivation of the *De* varies in degree from person to person. 'The man of the superior *De*' follows the *Dao* of spontaneity and never displays his *De* in any pretentious form. That is why he is 'not conscious of his *De*' but 'really possesses the *De*.' 'The man of the inferior *De*,' on the contrary, tends to hold a superficial attitude toward the *Dao*, and therefore keeps to the exhibitionist form of the *De*. That is why he 'never loses sight of his *De*' but has 'no true *De*.' Since he always takes action on selfish purpose, he is apt to achieve momentary gains but suffer long-term losses in most cases.

The idea that 'only when the *Dao* is lost does the *De* disappear' is derived from the rearranged line in Chinese *gu shi dao er shi de* according to the philological studies (Gu and Zhou, 1991: 278–9). This is actually based on the fact that the *Dao* and the *De* are inseparable by nature. The interrelation between them threads through Laozi's philosophical system. Yet, in some DDJ editions the line goes like this: 'Only when the *Dao* is lost does the *De* arise' (*gu shi dao er hou de*), which seems to make a distinction between the *Dao* and the *De* in the sense of time sequence on the one hand, and treats the *De* as a value paradigm independent of the *Dao* on the other. This seems to be logically problematic with regard to the entirety of Laozi's doctrine.

'The flower of the *Dao*' (*dao zhi hua*) can also be rendered as 'the ornament of the *Dao*,' figuratively signifying the appealing surface of the *Dao*. It is still far away from 'the fruit,' that is, the substantial truth of the *Dao*. 'The great man' stands for the Daoist sage. 'The thick' is explained by Heshang Gong in terms of 'simplicity, honesty and sincerity' (1991: 22). I think 'the thick' in this context refers to what is adequate, like the 'superior *De*,' while 'the thin' refers to what is inadequate, like the 'superior humanity' (*shang ren*), 'superior righteousness' (*shang yi*) and 'superior propriety' (*shang li*). As mentioned above, 'the fruit' symbolizes the substantial truth of the *Dao* whereas 'the flower' the appealing ornament of the *Dao*. In a word, Laozi encourages people to approach 'the superior *De*' as the truth of the *Dao* rather than 'the inferior *De*' as the ornament of the *Dao*.

Noticeably in this section as a whole, Laozi presents his hierarch of values comprising the 'superior *De*' and the 'interior *De*' as its two distinct categories. The former is highly recommended as the manifestation of the *Dao*. It is characterized by its adhesion to the principle of 'take-no-action' or the way of spontaneity. Likewise 'the man of the superior *De*' is an ideal personality to be imitated by all walks of life, for he is the one who has attained the genuine *Dao*.

In view of the latter, its elements go downward from 'superior humanity,' through 'superior righteousness' to 'superior propriety' which were officially appreciated by the ruling class then, and persistently advocated by the school of Confucianism ever since. If considered from Laozi's perspective, they all tend to deviate from the way of naturalness and principle of take-no-action no matter whether or not they aim at self-exhibition and favorable returns. Hence they may show inadequacy in doing this, and weakness in doing that; or worse still, they may be reduced to mere pretentious protocols which restricts their behavior and puts them in mental straitjackets. History has shown that it would be employed, more often than not, by self-seeking people.

Laozi expresses his preference for the 'superior *De*' for being symbolic of simplicity and sincerity in one sense, and corresponding to his philosophy of taking no imposing action in the other sense. At the same time, he tenders his critique of the 'inferior *De*' since it works the other way round. This also reflects his nostalgia for Daoist innocence and plainness, and his anxiety derived from his observation that social instability results from nothing but the damage to and desertion of the *Dao*, and meanwhile from the propagation and application of other low-brow values such as 'humanity' *(ren)*, 'righteousness' *(yi)*, and 'propriety' *(li)*, among others.

Incidentally, the hierarchical distinction between the *Dao*, *De*, humanity, righteousness and propriety is made in almost all the DDJ editions of 81 sections. Yet, this distinction is found nowhere in the Guodian DDJ version on bamboo slips, in which the *Dao* and other values aforementioned are corresponding to each other instead of being set out in contradiction (see 23.2).

Chapter 7

The Qualities of the De

The *De* functions in various domains due to its diversity of qualities. Similarly, it is cultivated and manifested in different manners, which all accord with the criteria of the *Dao*. The figurative comparison of the profound *De* to an innocent infant contributes to understanding the effects of the *De*. In this regard, Sections 54 and 55 (DDJ) deserve attention.

7.1 (Section 54)

He who is good at building cannot be shaken.
He who is good at holding can lose nothing.
Thus his ancestral sacrifice can pass down
    From generation to generation.
When cultivated and exercised in the person,
    The *De* will become pure and genuine.
When cultivated and exercised in the family,
    The *De* will become full and overflowing.
When cultivated and exercised in the common,
    The *De* will become constant and everlasting.
When cultivated and exercised nationwide,
    The *De* will become powerful and abundant.
When cultivated and exercised worldwide,
    The *De* will become universal and widespread.

Therefore (by taking it as a standard should we)
    Use this person to examine other persons,
    Use this family to examine other families,
    Use this community to examine other communities,
    Use this country to examine other countries.
    And use this world to examine other worlds.
How do I know the situation of all things under Heaven?
Precisely by the method above-mentioned.

Commentary

This section conveys a moral teaching Laozi offers chiefly to the lords, aristocrats, and ruling class at large. They will benefit a great deal provided they apply the *Dao* to their conduct of affairs.

The *De* is conceptualized as the manifestation and function of the *Dao*. When fostered and carried out in accordance with the *Dao*, the *De* features a wide variety of advantages in myriad realms. Judged respectively from the ethical and social perspectives, for instance, the *De* plays a significant part in the virtuous cultivation of the personality, proper regulation of the family, effective organization of the community, stable government of the country, and peaceful environment of the world.

Accordingly, the benefits and advantages originated from the *De* are confined to a handful of rulers and aristocrats, since the populace could not enjoy the sacrifices of their posterity. This is true to some degree. Yet, a scrutiny of the text in question leads one to discern Laozi's aim to radiate the *Dao* and the *De* from person to person, from family to family, from community to community, from country to country, until they are eventually spread far and wide all over the world. Only by so doing can the world be free from disorder and the people from suffering.

What is indicated by the line that 'thus his ancestral sacrifice can pass down from generation to generation' is the advantage of adhering to the *De* as a code of conduct outwardly and as the demonstration of the *Dao* in essence. If people are conscious of its significance when it comes to building and holding things, they will encounter no failure, loss, or frustration. Instead, they will enjoy continuity of a positive and constructive kind.

What is noteworthy in the last stanza is the distinction between 'this world' and 'other worlds.' In plain terms, 'this world' means the world where the *De* as the manifestation of the *Dao* is cultivated and exercised, while 'the other worlds' are ones where the *De* is not cultivated or exercised yet. In this context, it is the same with this person and other persons, this family and other families, this community and other communities, and this country and other countries.

7.2 (Section 55)

He who possesses the *De* in abundance
  Can be compared to a newborn infant.
Poisonous insects will not sting him.
Fierce brutes will not injure him.
Birds of prey will not attack him.
His bones are weak and his sinews tender,
  But his grasp is firm.
He does not yet know about the intercourse of male and female.

But his organ is aroused
  For his physical essence is at its height.
He may cry all day without becoming hoarse,
  For his innate harmony is simply perfect.
The essence and harmony as such are natural and constant.
To know this is called being wise.
The desire to multiply life's enjoyments means ill omen
The mind to employ vital energy excessively suffers fatal stiffness.
  Things that have grown strong commence to become old.
This is called 'being contrary to the *Dao*.'
Whatever is contrary to the *Dao* will soon perish.

Commentary

In this section, as has been observed by Ren Jiyu, 'Laozi preaches the philosophy of non-action as an attitude toward life, and teaches people to return to a state of primitive ignorance. He advocates being like an innocent child without desires. This accords with the criteria of the *Dao*, and one can avoid disasters by remaining weak, soft and ignorant, otherwise he will soon perish owing to his opposition to the principle of the *Dao*' (1993: 75).

Moreover, Laozi goes on to describe figuratively his philosophizing of self-preservation in a twofold sense: social and physical. If viewed from a social dimension, a newborn baby, weak and tender as it is, is free from attack by poisonous insects, fierce brutes, and birds of prey that are symbolic of the evil-natured who are always ready to cut down the good-willed. If a person was as ignorant and innocent as an infant without desires, he would live a life of his own without threatening the interests of anyone else. Therefore, he could avoid jealousy, hatred, and danger; or in other words, he could defend, passively or otherwise, and preserve himself. This well responds to the saying that 'ignorance is bliss.'

With regard to self-preservation in a physical sense, the fact that a newborn infant is taken as a model is largely due to the fact that it is filled with vitality and has not lost a single gram of its essential vital energy. An innocent child usually lives a natural life, different from adults who have strong desire and high life-consciousness. Laozi believes that 'the tender and the soft are companions of life,' and so is the child for sure. Hence, he who wants to preserve his physical life should follow the living state of infancy. In the final analysis, this state of being embodies the way of jauntiness and freedom from desires.

With regard to the material and bodily pleasure-seeking phenomena and related problems that we encounter nowadays, we can profit from Laozi's instruction as follows: 'the desire to multiply life's enjoyments means ill omen; the mind to employ vital energy excessively suffers fatal stiffness.'

Contextual studies inform us that Laozi's concept of light (*ming*) means 'wise' or 'wisdom,' while that of learning (*zhi*) means 'knowing' or 'knowledge.' This is testified by such sayings as 'he who knows others is learned; he who knows himself is wise' (*zhi ren zhe zhi, zi zhi zhe ming*) (DDJ, Sect. 33), 'this is called subtle wisdom' (*shi wei wei ming*) (DDJ, Sect. 36), and so on. From a Daoist viewpoint, any desire to increase life's enjoyments in a pleasure-seeking fashion will naturally harm and injure life itself. It is disastrous to add more to life's enjoyments as well as being against the way of spontaneity or naturalness in Laozi's thinking. Noticeably, the excessive use of *qi* as vital energy will inevitably lead to over-exhaustion and disharmony between *Yin* and *Yang* as two kinds of vital force in the body. The expression 'fatal stiffness' implies lack of vitality or physical decline. This is in line with Laozi's conviction that 'the hard and the stiff are companions of death' (DDJ, Sect. 76).

Chapter 8

On Have-Substance and Have-No-Substance

Laozi lived at a time of frequent warfare, power struggle, and greed-ridden materialism. Protesting the social reality as such, he never failed to gain insights into the crises of the human condition and the miseries from which people suffered in his day. The crises and miseries actually came from both outside (the environment) and inside (the ego). Sharp observations allow Laozi to propose some alternative solutions to the social ills. Many of his ideas still bear some relevance to the issues we contend with nowadays.

Distinct from Being-within-form and Being-without-form as defined in Section 1 (DDJ, see 1.1), Have-substance and Have-no-substance as a pair of concepts reflects Laozi's dialectical thinking in terms of their complementary interaction. Laozi seems to infuse more importance into Have-no-substance since he believes it to be more decisive in the aspects of utility and function. This is consistent with his general principle that 'Being-within-form comes from Being-without-form' on the one hand, and his idea of 'vacuity' (*xu*) for its receptivity and accommodativeness on the other hand. A textual analysis of Section 11 (DDJ) helps to illustrate the interrelations between Have-substance and Have-no-substance.

8.1 (Section 11)

Thirty spokes are united around the hub to make a wheel,
    But it is on the central hole for the axle
    That the utility of the chariot depends.
Clay is kneaded to mold a utensil,
    But it is on the empty space inside it
    That the utility of the utensil depends.
Doors and windows are cut out to form a room,
    But it is on the interior vacancy
    That the utility of the room depends.
Therefore, Have-substance brings advantage
    While Have-no-substance creates utility.

Commentary

As can be observed in this section, such expressions as 'the central hole,' 'the empty space,' and 'the interior vacancy' are concrete examples used to illustrate the concept of 'Have-no-substance.' This is often the case with Laozi's expression of abstract ideas. Importantly, 'Have-no-substance' is the English version for Laozi's idea of *wu*, distinct from the concept of Being-without-form (*Wu*) as has been analyzed earlier (see 1.1). The primary discrepancy between them is determined by the fact that the former is something blank or empty in contrast with something concrete around it, while the latter features the essence of the *Dao* that is invisible and intangible to sensory perception. In other words, 'Have-no-substance' is what can be apprehended from a spatial and phenomenal perspective, while Being-without-form is what can be conceived from an abstract or a metaphysical perspective. Under certain circumstances, 'Have-no-substance' can be rendered as Have-vacuity. Contrarily, 'Have-substance' as the rendering of *you* is different from Being-within-form as presented in Section 1 (DDJ, see 1.1). Although the same Chinese word (*you*) is used, its connotations are far apart. The former carries a physical sense tied to the phenomenal world, whereas the latter has a metaphysical sense related to the production and general principle of all things.

The subject matter of this section in the main intends to demonstrate the dialectical interrelationship between Have-substance and Have-no-substance, or advantage and utility. Laozi maintains that these two aspects are seemingly opposite. But they are counterparts, helping complete each other, and therefore remaining interdependent. Laozi emphasizes the importance of Have-no-substance which he thinks is the more decisive correlative. In view of this tendency, we should be aware of the fact that it is right for Laozi to underline the dialectical unity of Have-substance and Have-no-substance with regard to the advantage and utility of a chariot, utensil, and room, but wrong (or logically problematic at least) for him to elevate Have-no-substance as an absolute opposite to Have-substance. After all, Have-no-substance as an empty space in a bowl, cup, or house comes into effect as a consequence of the concrete Have-substance.

In most cases, we are inclined to focus on the concrete dimension of things when neglecting their discrete aspect. But Laozi is observant enough to bring out the hidden utility of the latter, which often seems to be useless in appearance. His thought-way contains a kind of significance which may help us to develop an all-sided view on the one hand, and creative thinking on the other hand.

Laozi is admittedly adept at using specific and familiar examples to illustrate theoretically abstract ideas, thus making his arguments both comprehensible and convincing. A wheel and its central hole, a bow and its empty space, and a room and its interior vacancy are all set side by side to justify the interaction between Have-substance and Have-no-substance. This may also help the reader better understand the *Dao* via the function of the *De*.

Incidentally, the idea that 'Have-substance brings advantage while Have-no-substance creates utility' (*you zhi yi wei li, wu zhi yi wei yong*) is also influential in Chinese arts. Have-substance (*you*) and Have-no-substance (*wu*) as two different but inseparable categories are closely associated with another pair known as 'the concretization in the painted part' (*shi*) and 'the abstraction in the blank part' (*xu*). 'The mutual production between the concretization and the abstraction' (*xu shi xiang sheng*) is applied as a general principle to art creation in the genres of Chinese traditional ink painting, calligraphy, opera, architecture, and horticulture, and even poetry. Further discussion is to be dealt with later in 12.1 (Section 2) with regard to the beautiful and the ugly.

Chapter 9

On Take-Action and Take-no-Action

Take-no-action is one of the essential features of the *Dao*. It is virtually a substitute expression for 'follow the way of spontaneity.' It is therefore recommended by Laozi as the ideal for political and governmental praxis since it facilitates the proper outcome. Conversely, take-action, as an opposite alternative, can be misleading and hindering owing to its imposed purposefulness and limited capacity, as has been discussed previously (see 6.2). In this connection, we will look into Sections 37 and 29 (DDJ).

9.1 (Section 37)

The *Dao* invariably takes no action,
　　And yet there is nothing left undone.
If kings and lords are able to maintain it,
　　All things will submit to them due to self-transformation.
If, after submission, they have resurging desires to act,
　　I should subdue them by the nameless simplicity.
When they are subdued by the nameless simplicity,
　　They will be free of desires.
Being free of desires, they will be tranquil,
　　And the world will of itself be rectified.

Commentary

According to Heshang Gong, that 'the *Dao* invariably takes no action' is a general principle of the *Dao* itself (1991: 21). The expression 'takes no action' is a rendering of Laozi's notion *wu wei*, which implies 'the way of following spontaneity' (*shun zi ran ye*) according to Wang Bi (1989: 9). It finds its equivalent in the expression 'doing nothing' in some DDJ versions. Yet, one must remember not to approach its meaning from a purely practical dimension. In plain terms, it should be understood as 'doing nothing of a forceful nature' or 'taking no unnecessary or blind action.' Hence Wing-tsit Chan explains that 'non-action (*wu-wei*) does not literally mean "inactivity" but "taking no action that is contrary to Nature," in other words, letting Nature take its own course' (1973: 136).

As can be noted in this section, Laozi is preoccupied with the human condition and intends to facilitate social stability and peace. Living in a drastically chaotic age, he has seen enough of the problems and sufferings caused by such actions as official decrees, taxation requirements, and repeated advocacy of such norms as 'humanity,' 'righteousness,' and 'propriety.' He himself opposes all these actions that tend to make things worse than better. He therefore advises the ruling class to act upon his supreme principle of 'take-no-action.' In fact, he blames all problems and sufferings on the ruling class, who are filled with power-hungry and achievement-oriented desires and ambitions *qua* a leading source of all social evils and ills. Thus they should be subdued by means of the *Dao* as is identified with the 'nameless simplicity.' Only by so doing can the ruling class become tranquil; only when they have become tranquil and realized the significance of 'take-no-action' will they desist from political intrigue and turbulence. Accordingly, Laozi envisages the diminution of all troubles once and for all, and consequently, government will be conducted in the right orbit, and peace and stability will be restored to the world. This idea finds similar expressions in Sections 2 and 45 (see 12.1 and 14.4).

The basic components of 'take-no-action' as the ultimate solution to all troubles encompass 'simplicity,' 'tranquility,' and, above all, 'elimination of desires.' These are all meant to encourage the ruling class to create a plain and simple living style for the whole of society, and remain free from any pursuit of personal gain or expansion of selfish wants. By acting upon these principles the rulers will benefit and live peacefully. This may as well make it possible for the ruled to live in the same fashion.

Another piece of advice offered to the ruling class lies in the principle of 'self-transformation' on the part of the populace in general. That is, the commoners should be left free to develop individually in their own way precisely because anything forced upon them would go astray in practice.

This point requires a further clarification. That is to say, by 'take-no-action' is meant that man should act and react as naturally as possible upon objective principles instead of imposing his subjective judgment onto other people or external things. So natural are such phenomena, for instance, as the growing of plants in the fields, the swimming of fish in the water, the sprouting of leaves on the willows, the flying of birds in the sky, and the blossoming of flowers in the garden or elsewhere. One should not bother them or interfere in their way of life. If he tries to 'pull the plants to make them grow faster,' or to 'take fish from the water to the land,' what would become of them then? In short, 'take-no-action' implies that man should do things in accordance with their individual natures and let them be what they can be. This reminds us of Zhuangzi, who continues this line of thought by means of illustrative examples. The duck's legs are short, for instance, but if man tries to lengthen them, the duck will feel pain. And similarly, the crane's legs are long, but if man tries to cut off a portion of them, the crane will also feel pain. Therefore, man should not shorten what is by nature long nor lengthen what is by nature short, because any modification of nature through externally forced action is unexceptionably the cause of pain and suffering. It is of frequent occurrence in this world that man takes actions to change the existing nature of things. He may assure himself of his good intentions, and yet, what he considers to be good may not be considered good by others. As a result, the actions one takes may violate the natural law and lead to something negative. It may be enlightening to consider one of Zhuangzi's parables: 'the emperor of the South Sea was called Shu; the emperor of the North Sea was called Hu; and the emperor of the Central Region was called Hundun. Shu and Hu from time to time came together for a meeting in the territory of Hundun, who always treated his two guests very generously. Shu and Hu discussed how they could repay his kindness. "All men," said they, "have seven holes for seeing, hearing, eating, and breathing. But Hundun alone has none of them. Let us try to bore some for him." So every day they bored one hole; but on the seventh day Hundun died' (Fung 1989: 113). The Chinese names of the three characters are virtually symbolic. Shu could mean 'change' or 'haste'; Hu could mean 'sudden' or 'speed'; and Hundun could mean 'chaos' or 'simplicity.' Shu and Hu could symbolize 'take-action' whereas Hundun could symbolize 'take-no-action.'

Nevertheless, the notion of 'take-no-action' has its negative impact owing to its literal interpretation and misconception. To be exact, when it is superficially interpreted as 'inactivity' or 'doing nothing' at all, it militates against human initiative; when it is mistaken as a way of waiting for one's luck, it seems to encourage patience and passiveness; when it is practically adopted as an approach to self-defense, it seems to call for irresponsibility or escapism from social commitment . . . As a consequence, 'take-no-action' in the distorted sense of this term is somewhat rooted as an element in the psychology of some Chinese people. Hence, they tend to shrink from difficulties, hardships, rebuffs, failures, and challenges. That is, the main reason why Lu Xun, China's leading twentieth century writer, severely attacked the doctrines of Laozi and Zhuangzi by labeling them as poisonous doses prescribed for passive and defensive beings.

It is worth mentioning the conclusion in Section 48 (DDJ) that 'if one likes to do anything arbitrary, he is not qualified to govern all under Heaven.' By the expression 'do anything arbitrary' (*you shi*) is meant 'take-action' (*you wei*) in Laozi's terminology. It is considered to be negative and disadvantageous in the long run, contrasting sharply with 'doing nothing' or 'take-no-action.' It should be made clear that 'doing nothing' or 'take-no-action' means doing whatever is not aimed at disturbing other people or going against the natural law in view of early Daoism. However, Laozi tends to absolutize the advantages of his favorite principle. That is why it is taken more often than not as meaning something extremely passive.

9.2 (Section 29)

I think that one will not succeed
　When he desires to govern All under Heaven and act upon it.
All under Heaven as a sacred vessel should not be acted upon,
　Nor should it be held on to.
He who acts upon it will harm it.
He who holds on to it will lose it.
Thus the sage takes no action, and therefore fails in nothing.
He holds on to nothing and therefore loses nothing.

Of all the creatures some lead and some follow;
　Some breathe and some blow;
　Some are strong and some are weak;
　Some rise up and some fall down.
Hence the sage discards the extreme,
　The extravagant and the excessive.

Meanwhile, he desires to have no desires.
He does not value rare treasures.
He learns what is unlearned
He returns to what is missed.
Thus he helps all things in natural development,
　But does not dare to take any action.

Commentary

In this section, Laozi directs his warning to the ruling class. He postulates that all things and people in the world have individual differences and distinct needs, even though they have something in common. They are characteristically independent so that they can hardly be governed by drastic measures that are imposed arbitrarily, nor can they be controlled by patternizing their conduct and ideology as the ruler wishes. Thus leadership of whatever kind cannot endure long if it fails to understand the above-mentioned situation. For this reason, Laozi subsequently offers his advice to follow the way of spontaneity and take no arbitrary action. Meanwhile, he expects the rulers to lead the people or govern the country by adroitly guiding actions according to circumstances (*yin shi li dao*).

　What is noteworthy here is the idea of 'All under Heaven' as a translation of *tian xia* that can also be rendered as 'the world' or 'the state.' It refers not only to the territory of the old Chinese empire in connection with a specific social institution or political system. Hence, a ruler cannot govern and control it according to his will alone. Nowadays, some modern scholars attempt to develop the notion of All under Heaven into a concept of cosmopolitanism by which it is meant the possible collaboration of shareholders in world affairs. This extension is largely a by-product of globalization. Even though it is found somewhat far-fetched, it remains good-natured and instructive at a time when all the nations are expected to join their efforts to handle global issues in economic, political, or environmental scopes. A special case is exemplified in the international treatment of the financial meltdown in 2008, for instance.

Chapter 10

On Pleasure-Snobbery and Acquisitiveness

It seems to be paradoxical that the progression of civilization tends to bring forth advantages and disadvantages at the same time. The situation was more or less the same in the past. Laozi persistently stresses the negative aspects of civilization in view of social ills. Based on his observation and anatomy of problematic reality in his time, his exposure of pleasure-snobbery and acquisitiveness sheds much light on the status quo of human existence. To be discussed here are Sections 12, 53, and 67 (DDJ).

10.1 (Section 12)

The five colors make one's eyes blind.
The five tones make one's ears deaf.
The five flavors dull one's palate.
Racing and hunting unhinge one's mind.
Goods that are hard to get tempt people to rob and steal.
Hence, the sage cares for the belly instead of the eyes;
And he rejects the latter but accepts the former.

Commentary

Literally speaking, 'the five colors' are yellow, green, red, white, and black. Here the expression means a rich variety of colors which appear sensuously dazzling. 'The five tones' of ancient Chinese music are known as *gong, shang, jue, zhi,* and *yu,* representing the five notes of the ancient Chinese five-tone scale. They correspond somewhat to 1, 2, 3, 5, and 6 in numbered musical notation. Here the expression means enjoyable and exciting music. 'The five flavors' are sweet, sour, bitter, pungent, and salty. Here the expression means sensuous delicacies. 'Racing and hunting' implies passionate or unbridled indulgence in entertainment. 'Goods that are hard to get' indicates treasures or valuables in particular, and wealth or property in general. 'The belly' signifies the possibility of easy contentment with what one has, while 'the eyes' stand for the insatiable desire for sensuous enjoyment.

With penetrating insight into materialistic civilization in general and sharp observation on the easy access the rich have to a luxurious way of life, Laozi levels criticism at pleasure-snobbery and wealth-oriented acquisitiveness as two overwhelming social problems encountered in his days. Things included in the categories of 'the five colors,' 'the five tones,' 'the five flavors,' 'goods that are hard to obtain,' and 'racing and hunting' are the major sources of pleasure and targets of acquisition. They are so tantalizing that those engrossed in them may fall into overindulgence. This will then lead to such detrimental consequences as distorted perception (i.e. dazzled eyes, deaf ears, and spoiled palate), mental imbalance (i.e. desire- and passion-riddenness), and aberrant behavior (i.e. robbery and theft). Hence, Laozi warns people (especially the rich) to rein in their pleasure-seeking and wealth-acquisition urges by caring for 'the belly instead of the eyes.'

As Chen Guying put it, to 'care for the belly means to regulate the inner life such that it remains tranquil, simple, and unruffled. To care for the eyes means to pursue a kind of outer life driven by greedy desires. The more one indulges in the latter, the more one gets engrossed in it and attached to it; accordingly, the more one will suffer from self-estrangement, the emptier one's soul will become. Therefore, Laozi asks people to get rid of external temptations, and to concentrate on peace of mind as well as inherent simplicity' (1992: 108).

Reconsidering these old ideas of Laozi, we can still feel their relevance to the reality today, and possibly sigh with regret at materialistic society given over to the pursuit of pleasure, wealth, and commodities. The rampant development of commercialism and materialism, for instance, can be attributed to greedy acquisitiveness: it is analogically similar to the extent that the more you drink Coca-Cola, the more thirsty you will become because 'you cannot beat the taste'; and likewise, as the rapid advance of the culture industry produces a variety of entertainment objects as dazzling and momentary as fireworks, the further you run after them, the further your taste will drop back.

Incidentally, it must be stressed that Laozi is not simply anti-art or anti-culture, as some scholars claim. He virtuously condemns the lavish way of life sought after by the rich on the one hand, and the potential dangers stirred up by acquisitive motives on the other hand. This intention can be proved by his advocacy of simplicity, contentedness, and freedom from desires throughout the DDJ text.

10.2 (Section 53)

If I have a little wisdom,
    I will walk along a broad way

And fear nothing but going astray.
The broad way is very even,
   But the powerful delight in by-paths.
The courts are exceedingly corrupt,
   Whereas the fields are exceedingly weedy
   And the granaries are exceedingly empty.
They are wearing elegant clothes,
   Carrying sharp swords,
   Enjoying exquisite food and drink,
   And owning abundant wealth and treasures.
They can be called robber chieftains.
   This is surely against the *Dao*.

Commentary

'The broad way' (*da dao*) denotes the right approach to either personal cultivation or state leadership which follows the *Dao*; 'by-paths' indicate the wrong or misleading approach which goes against the *Dao*. 'The powerful' signifies the rich and noble, and 'the courts' here stands for government in general.

In this section, Laozi openly attacks the powerful for their corruption of government, indulgence in excessive enjoyment, lavish vanity-snobbery, indifference to the common people, and, above all, exploitation of the people. Thus he expresses his indignation by calling them 'robber chieftains.'

According to Laozi, they live self-centered lives dominated by pleasure-seeking, and acquisitiveness due to the sheer fact that they refuse to 'walk along a broad way' but 'delight in by-paths.' That is to say, they prefer to take actions contrary to the supreme principle of the *Dao*. This is a fatal error, for such transgressors would not only lose what they once enjoyed, but also plunge themselves into jeopardy. We can collect more than sufficient evidence from history to show that any form of corrupted government and unjust property division tend to stir up uprisings or rebellions in all nations at all times.

10.3 (Section 67)

I have three treasures
   Which I grasp and keep.
The first is 'kindness.'
The second is 'frugality.'
The third is 'to dare not be ahead of the world.'

With kindness, one can become courageous.
With frugality, one can become generous.

With not daring to be ahead of the world,
  One can become the leader of the world.

Now it is a fatal mistake
  To seek courage by abandoning kindness,
  To seek generosity by abandoning frugality,
  And to seek precedence by abandoning retreat.
With kindness, one can be victorious in the case of attack,
  And remain firm in the case of defense.
Heaven will help and protect such a one through kindness.

Commentary

The 'three treasures' (*san bao*) are three virtues by nature. 'Kindness' is a rendering of *ci*, which also means love, affection, compassion, and even tolerance. 'Frugality' is a rendering of *jian*. Han Feizi interprets it by remarking that 'the wise man who uses his property frugally will have a well-off family; the sage who treasures his spirit will be full of energy' (Chen, 1992: 319). Because of frugality, one will not be lavish with one's wealth and will accordingly save up more; then he will be able to offer some to others. The fact of the matter is that 'frugality' as a kind of virtue has been recommended throughout Chinese history, as an approach to developing a well-off family or country. 'Courageous' is a rendering of *yong*, which also means brave or bravery. In this context, according to Jiang Xichang, that 'one can become courageous' means that one is liable 'to be modest, to compromise and to defend instead of competing, offending or invading' (Chen, 1992: 319).

Ren Jiyu assumes that 'this section specifically applies the principle of the *Dao* to politics and military affairs. Laozi introduces the so-called three precious things . . . and maintains that only the ability to fall back is bravery, the ability to shrink is to stretch, and that avoiding prominence and precedence makes one come first. Breach of the three principles will bring complete failure' (1993: 88).

Sha Shaohao criticizes Laozi for setting forth such three treasures as 'kindness,' 'frugality,' and 'not daring to be ahead of the world,' and seeming to have them all absolutized. Thus 'retreat' or 'defense' turns into an unalterable and supreme principle, and accordingly 'courage,' 'generosity,' and 'precedence,' and 'advance,' are neglected. The idea of precedence or daring to be ahead of the world plays virtually a leading role in the process of development. This proves that Laozi deviates here from his normal dialectical approach (1992: 136).

Apart from the above-mentioned observations, it can be said that Laozi offers his three treasures in respect to the social problems of his time, problems that involve rampant pleasure-snobbery, insatiable acquisitiveness and harsh competition among the people in general, and the rich and powerful in particular. He warns them in no uncertain terms that those who go against the three treasures as an interrelated code of conduct are doomed to failure and disaster. With regard to the three treasures, the last two (i.e. frugality and precedence) seem directed toward self-preservation and self-defense, while the first (i.e. kindness) toward spiritual nourishment. In addition, it seems to be of universal significance, for kindness can never be enough in the competitive world we happen to live in, now as then.

Chapter 11

On the Hard and the Soft

It seems to be a universal rule that the strong conquer the weak, and correspondingly, the hard overwhelm the soft. However, Laozi thinks in reverse from a dynamic and dialectical perspective. He grounds his philosophy of keeping to the soft and the tender upon his empirical observation of natural changes. Plain and simplistic as his thinking may be, his method of reverse speculation remains fairly instructive even today. Sections 43, 76, and 78 (DDJ) tell about this argument.

11.1 (Section 43)

The softest thing in the world
   Runs in and out of the hardest thing.
The invisible force penetrates any creviceless being.
Thereby I come to know the advantage of take-no-action.
Few in the world can realize the merits of wordless teaching
   And the benefits of doing nothing.

Commentary

It is noticeable that Laozi here propounds the view that the soft and the weak overcome the hard and the strong, and the advantages that come from 'take-no-action.' Meanwhile, he proposes his philosophy of compromising for the sake of gaining more, and of retreating for the sake of advancing further.

This could also be taken as advice to the strong and powerful for they tend to be short-sighted, arrogant, or self-important. It is well to keep in mind the fact that things are always on the move, developing into their opposites and replacing one another naturally. Therefore, historically sedimented in the Chinese psychology is a distinct understanding of the interactions between 'the strong and the soft,' 'the firm and the yielding,' 'advance and retreat,' and 'contract and expand.' In the 'Commentary on the Appended Phrases' in *The*

Classic of Changes (*Yi jing xi ci zhuan*), one may read with enlightenment the following: 'When the eight trigrams (*ba gua*) formed ranks, the [basic] images were present there within them . . . When they let the hard and the soft [i.e. the strong and the weak, the unyielding and the yielding, the *yang* and *yin* trigrams] displace each other, change was present within them . . . Thanks to constancy, the *Dao* of the sun and the moon makes them bright. Thanks to constancy, all the activity that takes place in the world is the expression of the One . . . When the sun goes, then the moon comes; and when the moon goes, then the sun comes. The sun and the moon drive each other on, and brightness is generated in this process. When the cold goes, then the heat comes; and when the heat goes, then the cold comes. The cold and the heat drive each other on, and the yearly seasons come into being in this process. What has gone is a contraction, and what is to come is an expansion. Contraction and expansion impel each other; and benefits are generated in this process. The contraction of the measuring worm is done in order to try to stretch itself out, and the hibernation of dragons and snakes is done in order to preserve their lives. Perfect concepts [*jingyi*] come about by entrance into the numinous [*ru shen*], which, once had, allow one to extend their application to the utmost. The use of these applications comes about by making one's person secure, which allows for the subsequent exaltation of his virtue' (Lynn, 1994: 75–82). Noticeably, the movement of the measuring worm is symbolic of the interaction between retreat (drawing itself together) and advance (stretching out); and similarly, the habit of dragons and snakes are symbolic of the interaction between tranquility (hibernating in a static sense) and motion (preserving life in a dynamic sense). By 'perfect concepts' is meant 'the profound subtlety of the principle of things.' By 'the numinous,' being utterly still, is meant not to act, but its response to something is perfect and thoroughgoing. If properly considered and applied, all this will serve to bring forth benefits and advantages, and above all, the exaltation of personal virtues (*de*).

11.2 (Section 76)

When alive, man is soft and tender.
After death, he is hard and stiff.
All things like grass and trees are soft and tender when alive,
   Whereas they become withered and dried when dead.
Therefore, the hard and the stiff are companions of death
   Whereas the soft and the tender are companions of life.
Hence an army will be shattered when it becomes strong.
A tree will be broken when it grows huge.
The hard and the strong fall in the inferior position;
The soft and the tender stay in the superior position.

'The violent and the strong do not die natural deaths.'
I shall take this principle as the father of my teaching.

Commentary

In this section, Laozi cites a number of handy and approachable examples drawn from natural phenomena and military operations. He employs them to reinforce his notion that the soft and the tender are the most potential and powerful, whereas the hard and the strong are the most fragile and teeter on the brink of termination or destruction. This manifests the fact that Laozi tends to view things in respect of their intrinsic development and change. In effect, his dialectical thinking bears an insight into the dynamic interaction between the opposite facets of all things, which is already implied by the well-known generalization presented in Section 40 that 'Reversion is the movement of the *Dao*. Weakness is the function of the *Dao*' (see 3.1).

It is also discernable that Laozi clings to a skeptical viewpoint all the way through. He reverses against all certainties with regard to the positive values overwhelmingly celebrated in the society of his time. Hence his ideas appear to be antithetical to either established norms or accepted logic. However, one should never fail to neglect the absolutization of the conviction that the soft and the tender are bound to conquer the hard and the strong, which threads through Laozi's doctrine. Such absolutization cuts 'the soft and the tender' off from any other variables or possible influences, thus making a certainty out of the negation of other certainties or values positively socialized and appreciated during that period.

'The violent and the strong do not die natural deaths' implies that when an army becomes strong it tends to be aggressive and longs to show off its strength by attacking others. By so doing it runs the risk of weakening itself and finally being destroyed. A fully grown tree is likely to be felled for it is buffeted by more wind in a storm, or it is cut down for timber owing to its tremendous usefulness. Like a strong army ready to display its power, the violent and strong will soon meet their doom instead of a natural end. 'The father of my teaching' indicates the root, foundation, beginning, or general principle of Laozi's teaching.

11.3 (Section 78)

Nothing in the world is softer and weaker than water,
    But no force can compare with it in attacking the hard and the strong.
For this reason there is no substitute for it.
Everyone in the world knows
    That the soft can overcome the hard,

And the weak can overcome the strong,
  But none can put it into practice.
Therefore the sage says;
'He who shoulders the disgrace for his nation
  Can be the sovereign of the country;
  He who bears the misfortune of his nation
  Can be the king of the world.'
Positive words seem to be their opposite.

Commentary

As has been detected by many readers and Laozi scholars, this section highlights once again the character of water. Water appears soft and weak, but it can bring down hard and strong things alike. From this natural phenomenon Laozi infers that softness, weakness, and humbleness are conducive to gains instead of losses. A wise ruler should apparently keep to himself all humiliation or disgrace by being as humble as water itself. Thus he seems to be in the lowest place, but in fact he stays in a high position above the others in view of the potential power concerned.

Noticeably, Laozi recommends the function of water which is metaphorically used to schematize the characteristics of the *Dao* and the *De* in his terminology. Water seems to enjoy such positive features as follows: first and foremost, it is beneficial to the growth of all things in the world. Secondly, it is not competitive with others. Thirdly, it goes down to the lower places and tends to keep an appearance of humbleness. Finally, being a symbol of the soft and the weak, it has such great potential power that it can well defeat the hard and the strong. And this potential power is largely determined by the perseverance or persistent character of water itself. Viewing the text as a whole, we can safely conclude that Laozi's depiction of water in terms of its function reflects his philosophy of 'sticking to the soft and the tender' on the one hand, and on the other, accords with his principle that 'Weakness is the function of the *Dao*.'

It is worth mentioning that the image of water is also figuratively used by Sunzi, a contemporary of Laozi. In his well-known book titled *The Art of War* (*Sunzi bing fa*), he writes that 'the laws of military operations are like water; the tendency of water is to flow from heights to lowlands. The law of successful operations is to avoid the enemy's strength and strike his weakness. Water changes its course in accordance with the contours of the land. The soldier works out his victory in accordance with the situation of the enemy. Hence, just as water retains no constant shape, so in war there are no constant conditions. He who can modify his tactics in accordance with the enemy situation and thereby succeeds in winning may be said to be divine' (1993: 41–42).

That 'positive words seem to be their opposite' is a rendering of *zheng yan ruo fan* as one of the essential concepts propounded by Laozi. According to an annotation made by Heshang Gong, 'positive words' (*zheng yan*) means upright words that tell the truth. Yet, they cannot be rightly conceived or understood by ordinary people as they are mistaken for something negative, wrong or absurd (1991: 43). Relevant instances are easily found in the DDJ, such as 'the soft can overcome the hard, and the weak can overcome the strong' (Section 78); 'an army will be shattered when it becomes strong, and a tree will be broken when it grows huge' (Section 76); 'what is most full seems to be empty . . . The most straight seems to be crooked; the greatest skill seems to be clumsy; the greatest eloquence seems to be stammering' (Section 45); 'The *Dao* that is bright seems to be dark; the *Dao* that goes forward seems to retreat; the *Dao* that is level seems to be uneven; the lofty *De* looks like a humble valley; the greatest glory looks like a disgrace . . .' (Section 41).

Chapter 12

On the Beautiful and the Ugly

As regards the distinction between the beautiful and the ugly, Laozi's treatise is characterized by relativity and mutualism. This is seen to be based on his observation that there are always two opposites in everything. These two opposites contrast and complete each other. Thus one cannot do without the other due to their mutuality and, likewise, one cannot exist without the other either. Here we make particular reference to Section 2 (DDJ).

12.1 (Section 2)

When the people of the world know the beautiful as beauty,
  There arises the recognition of the ugly.
When they know the good as good,
  There arises the recognition of the evil.

This is the reason why
  Have-substance and have-no-substance produce each other;
  Difficult and easy complete each other;
  Long and short contrast with each other;
  High and low are distinguished from each other;
  Sound and voice harmonize with each other;
  Front and back follow each other.

Thus, the sage conducts affairs through take-no-action;
  He spreads his doctrines through wordless teaching;
  He lets all things grow without his initiation;
  He nurtures all things but takes possession of nothing;
  He promotes all things but lays no claim to his ability;
  He accomplishes his work but takes no credit for his contribution.
It is because he takes no credit
  That his accomplishment stays with him for ever.

Commentary

This section stresses that everything features a unity of two opposites. The fact of the matter is that if we try to approach and evaluate conceptually what surrounds us, we often find a tendency to classify almost all things in terms of their respective values and contradictive aspects. Thus there emerge antithetical concepts in binary pairs, such as beautiful and ugly, good and evil, have-substance and have-no-substance, difficult and easy, long and short, high and low, front and back. Their interactions can be largely boiled down to the characteristics of bilateral opposition and paradoxically mutual production as exist in the phenomenal world. In other words, they come into being in a relative, contrasting, and, above all, interdependent mode.

In view of the beautiful and the ugly, they are two antithetical categories associated with judgment. They come into being in pairs and in mutual contrast. In plain terms, what is considered beautiful is so because of the contrast with what is considered ugly, and vice versa. It is the same with the good and the evil. From his dialectical perspective, Laozi observes that the beautiful and the ugly are brought into being in the process of value judgment through comparison and contrast. That is to say, they are different but not absolutely antithetical to or incompatible with each other. They seem to have no positive hiatus between them. They are in effect interlinked to the extent that they co-exist or set off each other. This argument can be well justified by a statement in Section 20 (DDJ): 'how much difference is there between the beautiful and the ugly?' (*mei zhi yu e, xiang qu ruo he*). This Chinese expression is also rendered as 'how much difference is there between the good and the evil?' for 'beautiful' (*mei*) and 'good' (*shan*) are sometimes used interchangeably as ethical terms, and so are 'ugly' (*e*) and 'evil'. Contrary to other philosophers like Confucius, who tends to make a clear-cut discrimination between the beautiful and the ugly, Laozi develops an insight into the relativity and changeability of the two categories, such that he refuses to absolutize the apparent opposition between them. Further evidence can be cited from Section 58 (DDJ): 'the normal can suddenly turn into the abnormal; the good can suddenly turn into the evil' (*zheng fu wei qi, shan fu wei yao*).

After all, Laozi's dialectical stance toward the beautiful and the ugly is of a negative kind, often leading to relativism. According to Li Zehou and Liu Gangji, this relativism does not lie in the fact that the two categories concerned form a contrast, but instead in the intention to erase the discrepancy between them. Under each circumstances people can easily become adaptable to the confusing reality and hold on to an attitude toward life which goes beyond the distinction between what is regarded as beautiful and what is regarded as ugly (1984: 213). This attitude is notably stated in Section 20 (DDJ): 'The multitude are so brilliant and self-exhibiting, I alone seem to be lost in darkness and ignorance. The multitude are so observant and discriminating, I alone intend to make no distinctions.' Thus, compared to the Confucianists' persistent pursuit of the beautiful (good) and moral campaign against the ugly (evil) even at the expense of life, Laozi's position is relatively negative and therefore less commendable.

On the other hand, it is an oversimplification to assert that Laozi attempts to completely deny and eliminate the distinction between the beautiful and the ugly. It seems more accurate to say that he advocates a rather indifferent attitude to such a distinction, even though he is highly conscious of its existence. The main reason for this lies in the hard fact that Laozi himself could not do anything about it during his harsh era when power and wealth spoke far more loudly than anything else. Hence, he deliberately ignores the distinction even though the populace clings to it in most cases.

However self-deceiving and self-contained his stance may be, Laozi never gives up in practice the search for the beautiful in the genuine sense of this term. In his conception, what is really beautiful is attributed to simplicity, naivety, plainness, quietude, tranquility, and purposelessness. It is, in a word, equal to and identified with his concept of the *Dao*. One is able to get into the perfect realm of real beauty only when he has ridded himself of enslavement by external things and obtained authentic freedom of the spirit. That is to say, he has realized the essential significance of the *Dao* at this stage. In addition, Laozi takes a skeptical view of the mundane discrimination between the beautiful and the ugly. Take his criticism of the rich and powerful for example. They lived lavishly and abandoned themselves to the 'five colors,' 'five tones,' and 'five flavors' (DDJ, Sect. 12), which were seen in their eyes as something sensuously beautiful and enjoyable. But Laozi looks upon them as something destructive and detrimental to the health. Furthermore, 'wearing elegant clothes, carrying sharp swords, enjoying exquisite food and drink . . .' (DDJ, Sect. 53) were considered beautiful by the nobility, but appeared to Laozi as something dangerous and pernicious. Therefore, he indignantly calls the self-indulgent possessors of those things 'robber chieftains.'

In the final analysis, Laozi, judging from either a skeptical or relativistic perspective, tends to maintain that what is taken as beautiful or ugly by the multitude turns out to be insignificant, valueless, relative, and contrastive. They can be interchangeable or reducible to one another, and those who dote on them are deviating from the *Dao* that is the one and only source of what is really beautiful to Laozi himself.

By the way, Laozi likes to recommend the virtue of 'wordless teaching' (*bu yan zhi jiao*), indicating in this context that the education of the people in general should be carried out without formal rules, regulations, or compulsory supervision, but instead, through imperceptible guidance and influence. Besides, 'wordless teaching' may, in Laozi's mind, suggest both a discouragement of governmental administration that resorts to a train of orders and a negation of the national education that relies on a kind of ideology. Related to this virtue are such essential qualities of the Daoist sage as 'taking possession of nothing' (*fu you*), 'laying no claim to his ability' (*fu shi*), and 'taking no credit for his contribution' (*fu ju*). These qualities are meant to encourage people to do, create, and give what they can. At the same time people are advised to reduce their desire for possessing things, exhibiting their abilities, and glorifying their achievements. This is precisely because all social conflicts, man-to-man clashes and even warfare, are, in Laozi's opinion, derived from personal (i.e. among the ruling class in particular) desires and ambitions in the scopes of demonstrating their competence, enlarging their property, and expanding their territory. Needless to say, these desires and ambitions will lead naturally to contest, competition, and even military action and counteraction.

Chapter 13

On Beauty, Truth, and Goodness

Laozi's exposition of beauty, truth, and goodness features his dialectical and skeptical thinking. His insight into the contradictions among the three values is penetrating, and his critique of the pretentiousness and artificiality is still enlightening even today. The unity of the three values seems to Laozi to be only possible in the *Dao* and not in a society imbued with craftiness and deception. Let us examine Sections 81 and 62 (DDJ).

13.1 (Section 81)

True words are not beautiful.
Beautiful words are not true.
A good man is not an eloquent arguer.
An eloquent arguer is not a good man.
He who knows does not show off his extensive learning.
He who shows off his extensive learning does not know.

Commentary

According to the philological research done by Ma Xulun and Gu Di, transposed to Section 77 (DDJ) is the second stanza of Section 81 that usually begins with 'The sage does not accumulate for himself . . .' (see 5.1). The binary pairs of concepts are employed here to justify the Daoist judgment. As a rule, 'true words' (*xin yan*) are so plain, sincere, and straightforward that they do not allow any rhetorical polishing or adorning. Therefore, they often appear to be flat and displeasing. Conversely, 'beautiful words' (*mei yan*) are so carefully chosen and modified that they are generally fine sounding and inviting. However, they are usually meant to either cover up what is true or mix up the true, the false and even the mendacious. 'A good man' (*shan zhe*) is fairly close in meaning to a Daoist sage. He is supposed to pursue the truth of the *Dao* alone. Having attained it by chance, he will maintain it without arguing about what it is or how it is possible. For the attainment of the *Dao* is a personal experience and perception rather than a verbal description. This mode of conduct and attitude is strikingly distinct from that of 'an eloquent arguer' (*bian zhe*), because the latter tends to be an exhibitionist who pretends to know when he does not really know the truth of the *Dao* proper.

It is noteworthy that in Chinese culture 'words' (*yan*) include sayings, speeches, discourses, and writings in general. They are seen as a reflection not only of style, but also as a mirror of personality. This naturally corresponds to the convention that 'one's literary works can be intrinsically identified with one's personality (*wen ru qi ren*).' Hence, the discussion of beauty, truth, and goodness in this context contains both a rhetorical and ethical sense. Of these values truth is implicitly the most crucial and decisive as it derives from the *Dao* on the one hand, and on the other, Laozi himself firmly opposes whatever is false and pretentious.

Laozi's ideas about beauty, truth, and goodness could be misleading to the extent that the reader may hurry to conclude that Laozi wrongly opposes the unity of the three values. The fact of the matter is that his ideas are an extension of his skeptical view of the relativity between the beautiful and the ugly. He grounds his observation and generalization on his critical and somewhat cynical stance vis-à-vis civilization as a whole, because civilization, in his eyes, 'rejects the great *Dao*' and gives rise to 'great hypocrisy' (DDJ, Sect. 18). Consequently in an unfavorable social climate, luxury-acquisitiveness and pleasure-snobbery squeeze out simplicity and genuineness, beautiful or sweet words are coined to conceal evil-natured intentions or motives, and eloquence is held in esteem at the cost of the pursuit of supreme truth and wisdom related to the *Dao*. In short, the significance of Laozi's critique of civilization lies in the antithetical relationship between beauty and truth as well as beauty and goodness.

Laozi points out that the three categories of beauty, truth, and goodness can never become unified into one due to the problems arising from civilization and the human condition. However, they can become inseparable if they are identified with the *Dao*. This is, according to Laozi, only possible in his ideal society free from all the problems mankind has always confronted throughout history. As can be asserted, Laozi bases his conception of beauty, truth, and goodness on the fundamental principle of the *Dao*. His criticism of 'beautiful words,' 'eloquent arguer,' and 'he who shows off his extensive learning' is largely directed at the pretentious and hypocritical aspects of what are commonly termed humanity, benevolence, righteousness, and so forth. The possibility of the unity of beauty, truth, and goodness merely relies on the insightful perception and achievement of the *Dao*. As regards the DDJ text itself, Liu Xie (c. 465–532) comments, 'Laozi abhorred dishonesty, so he said, "fine-sounding words are untrue." But his own book of five thousand characters is full of subtle beauty. He did not ignore art after all' (2003: 441).

However, Laozi is again found to have absolutized the opposition between beauty and truth as well as beauty and goodness. This shows the intuitive, simplistic, and also lop-sided aspect of his dialectics. It is definitely arbitrary to oversimplify in such a manner the diversified and complicated phenomena. Generalizations are not to lead one to become mired in mechanical metaphysics rather than active dialectics, thus arriving at such dogmatic conclusions as 'true words are not beautiful,' 'beautiful words are not true,' 'a good man is not an eloquent arguer,' 'an eloquent arguer is not a good man,' 'he who knows does not show off his learning,' 'he who shows off his learning does not really know,' and so forth.

13.2 (Section 62)

The *Dao* is the storehouse of all things.
It is treasured by the good man,
And also preserved by the bad man.

Honored words can gain respect from others.
    Fine deeds can have an impact on others.
Even if a man is bad,
    Why should he be ever rejected?
Therefore, the sage is always good at saving men,
    And consequently nobody is rejected.
He is always good at saving things,
    And consequently nothing is rejected.
This is called the hidden light.
Therefore, the good man is the teacher of the bad.
And the bad is the material from which the good may learn.
He who does not value the teacher
    Or care for the material,
    Will still be greatly deluded
    Though he thinks himself clever.
Such is called the significant subtlety of the *Dao*.
Therefore, on the occasion of enthroning an emperor
    Or installing the three ministers,
    It is better to offer the *Dao* as a present
    Though there are grand ceremonies of saluting them
    With the round jadeware, followed by the four-horse chariot.

Why did the ancients value this *Dao* so much?
Did they not say, 'Those who seek shall attain and
    Those who sin shall be freed?'
    For this reason it is valued by All under Heaven.

Commentary

As can be discerned, the lines from 'Therefore, the sage is always good . . .' to 'such is called the significant subtlety of the *Dao*' are moved here from Section 27 (DDJ) according to Gu Di's textual analysis (1991: 496–509). They are meant to interpret the idea that 'Even if a man is bad, why should he be ever rejected?' Laozi is obviously idealistic in respect of human education and behavioral modification. This notion has later become mingled with the principles of Chinese *Zen* Buddhism: 'Try to forgive and save all living creatures,' 'Remember to be always kind and charitable to all beings,' and so on. Hence there arose subsequently a popular Chinese saying that 'A murderer can be transformed into a Buddha as soon as he puts down his sword.'

As is read in this section, it sets out the assumption that 'The *Dao* is the storehouse of all things.' That is to say, the *Dao* is the source of beauty, truth, good, and everything else. It is treasured by both good and bad people precisely because it functions as an all-embracing principle and helpful guidance, such that it treats all men alike and offers protection to them all without any reservation or condition. Hence, the *Dao* can be widely recognized and valued if it is clarified and promoted by 'honored words' and 'fine deeds.' Such words and deeds are what the Daoist sage performs in accordance with the *Dao*. They are highly positive and symbolic of beauty and goodness between which there is no conflict at all. This is a result of their assumed unity or identity with the *Dao*. In striking contrast, beauty, goodness, and truth would remain subject to doubts and contradictions in a civilized society, as Laozi believes.

It is interesting to notice that Laozi and Confucius do not see eye to eye on this point. Laozi insists on a negative attitude; he plays down such human values as truth, beauty, and goodness, and meanwhile denies any ray of hope for their practical unity. On the contrary, Confucius persists in a positive attitude; he tries to affirm and advocate the possible unity of the human values. In short, 'Laozi looks at the problems of beauty, truth and goodness from a critical perspective of social civilization . . . His negative remarks about these social values are not purely inactive and ephemeral. They actually lay bare the historical fact that the clashes and incompatibilities between values are universally and chronically in existence in civilized society. In principle they demonstrate Laozi's individual insight into the problematic kernel of the society of his day, as well as his critical spirit with regard to its dark side' (Li and Liu, 1984: 217).

As for the saying that 'those who seek shall attain and those who sin shall be freed,' it indicates again the all-embracing nature of the *Dao* as rejects nobody. To be exact, the first part of the statement is meant to explain that *Dao* is easily available and attainable, providing that it is sincerely pursued; and the second part contains a hidden message that the *Dao* is able to help the misguided or sinners to turn into a new leaf. All this intends to create an open space for all beings to take up self-transformation by acting upon the *Dao*.

Chapter 14

On Modesty and Retreat

Modesty as a virtue has all along been appreciated and recommended in the history of Chinese thought and ethics. It is not only practically desirable in social life for the sake of human relations, but also spiritually indispensable with regard to self-cultivation and self-preservation. As for the doctrine of retreat in contrast to that of advance, it does not encourage people to withdraw from society, as is often misconceived. Instead, it advises people not to flaunt intelligence and successes, as this will surely bring about disaster. These themes are notably presented in Sections 8, 9, 24, and 45 (DDJ).

14.1 (Section 8)

The supreme good is like water.
Water is good at benefiting all things
    And yet it does not compete with them.
It dwells in places that people detest,
    And thus it is so close to the *Dao*.
In dwelling, (the best man) loves where it is low.
In the mind, he loves what is profound
In dealing with others, he loves sincerity.
In speaking, he loves faithfulness.
In governing, he loves order.
In handling affairs, he loves competence.
In his activities, he loves timeliness.
Since he does not compete,
    He is free from any fault.

Commentary

Laozi is fond of using the image of water to suggest such virtues as modesty, selflessness, and non-competition. Water appears humble, always flowing down to and dwelling in the low places. It remains selfless, always benefiting all things without competing with them. However, it is potentially powerful enough to overcome whatever is hard and strong. According to Laozi, nothing in the world is softer and weaker than water, but no force can compare with it in attacking the hard and strong. For this reason there is no substitute for it (see 11.3). Hence the ideal personality is expected to embody these qualities of water. As observed in reality, only those who take up what others are reluctant to do are most likely to succeed either in their career or personal development.

14.2 (Section 9)

To talk too much will lead to a quick demise.
Hence, it is better to keep to tranquility.
To keep what is full from overflowing
    Is not as good as to let it be.
If a sword-edge is sharpened to its sharpest,
    It will not be able to last long.
When your rooms are filled with gold and jade,
    You will not be able to keep them safe.
If you become arrogant because of honor and wealth,
    It will bring upon you misfortune.
Retreat as soon as the work is done.
Such is the *Dao* of Heaven.

Commentary

The first two lines are transposed from Section 5 (DDJ) in accordance with Gu Di's philological research (1991: 189–190). They seem to fit into this context and are thus offered as an advice for those who talk too much but do too less. This easily reminds us of Laozi's criticisms against the negative aspects of 'beautiful words' and 'an eloquent arguer.'

This entire section here reflects a moderate attitude toward social life, external things, and personal cultivation. It encourages people to become modest instead of showy and arrogant, to be contented instead of greedy and demanding, and to retreat in a timely fashion instead of advancing blindly. Otherwise, one will be liable to get into trouble and lose what he has already achieved.

By 'retreat' is not meant withdrawal from society and retiring into the mountains as a hermit. Its implication lies in the *De*, which does not allow one to show off what he has accomplished in one sense, and in another, not claim to be a higher achiever than others. For it is in Laozi's mind that any self-importance or self-expansion as a result of personal success will turn out to be a cause of failure or destruction in the end.

14.3 (Section 24)

He who stands on tiptoe is not steady.
He who doubles his stride cannot go far.
He who displays himself is not wise.
He who justifies himself is not prominent.
He who boasts of himself is not given any credit.
He who feels self-important is not fit for leadership.
From the perspective of the *Dao*,
　These are like remnants of food and tumors of the body,
　So disgusting that the one with the *Dao* stays away from them.
Likewise the sage knows himself but does not display himself.
He loves himself but does not feel self-important.
Hence he rejects that and accepts this.

Commentary

This section features a figurative expression of the demerits of self-display, self-opinion, self-exaggeration, and self-importance, which are likened to 'the remnants of food and tumors of the body.' It is noticeable that Laozi strongly detests arrogance and exhibitionism, as contrasted with modesty as an important virtue of human conduct and a possibility of realizing the truth of the *Dao*.

As regards the first two lines – 'He who stands on tiptoe is not steady. He who doubles his stride cannot go far,' we find that the former serves as advice to those who are so vain as to stand out from others while neglecting both the objective and subjective conditions; the latter warns those who are eager for quick success and instant benefit. In addition, they also imply Laozi's dialectical viewpoint that one should remain modest in order to establish oneself, and should retreat in order to advance. It is often proved in practice that there is some truth in what Laozi says.

By the way, the lines from 'Likewise the sage knows himself . . .' to the end of the section are transposed to Section 72 (DDJ) according to Gu Di's analysis (1991: 235–236). In the last line, by 'that' is meant self-display and self-importance, and by 'this' self-knowledge and self-love in the sense of self-preservation of body and spirit. This conclusion is bolstered by reference to Section 38, at the end of which Laozi remarks: 'The man of foreknowledge has but the flower of the *Dao* and is at the beginning of ignorance. Hence the great man dwells in the thick instead of the thin. He dwells in the fruit instead of the flower. Therefore he rejects the latter and accepts the former' (see 6.2).

14.4 (Section 45)

What is most perfect seems to be incomplete,
  But its utility cannot be impaired.
What is most full seems to be empty,
  But its utility cannot be exhausted.
The most straight seems to be crooked.
The greatest skill seems to be clumsy.
The greatest eloquence seems to stutter.

The tranquil overcomes the hasty.
The cold overcomes the hot.
By remaining quiet and tranquil,
  One can become a model for all the people.

Commentary

The first stanza of this section reveals some essential aspects of the ideal personality in early Daoism. They appear considerably different from what they really are. This observation reflects Laozi's dialectical thought, and his proposed approach to personal cultivation. As noticed, the actualization of the idealized personality is first of all dependent on the *De* of modesty and the philosophy of retreat.

The second stanza is mainly associated with the dialectical interaction between 'the tranquil' and 'the hasty.' The former can overcome the latter because tranquility leads to calmness, sharp observation, good reasoning, and, above all, wisdom. The notion of tranquility and its advantages advocated by Laozi are linked to his principle of 'take-no-action' in view of its deep structure.

Incidentally, in many other DDJ versions one comes across with the expression *zao sheng han* that could be rendered as 'rapid walking overcomes cold.' It appears, in my opinion, somewhat perplexing and superficial in this case. I personally agree with Jiang Xichang, Yan Lingfeng, and Chen Guying, who change it to *jing sheng zao* that means 'the tranquil overcomes the hasty' (Chen, 1992: 241), because it is logically appropriate for both the context and Laozi's entire system. The same idea is also expressed in Section 26 (DDJ) by the statement, 'the tranquil is the lord of the hasty' (*jing wei zao jun*). Wang Bi explains that 'the hasty is conducive to trouble while the tranquil is conducive to complete genuineness' (1989: 11).

Chapter 15

On Knowledge and Wisdom

Laozi makes a distinction between general knowledge and true wisdom. He holds a negative stance on the former, as he thinks it could be possibly superficial and even pretentious. But he gives much credit to the latter because he assumes it to be closely associated with the *Dao* as the origin of all things. It is observable that his proposed approach to wisdom features honesty, modesty, purity, sincerity, self-knowledge, and simplicity. To be scrutinized with regard to this theme are Sections 33, 47, 52, 56, and 71 (DDJ).

15.1 (Section 33)

He who knows others is knowledgeable.
He who knows himself is wise.
He who conquers others is physically strong.
He who conquers himself is really mighty.
He who is contented is rich.
He who acts with persistence has a will.
He who does not lose his root will endure.
He who dies but is not forgotten enjoys longevity.

Commentary

This section is a generalization of Laozi's philosophy on human existence. The ideas are presented in the form of contrast and comparison. It is rather difficult, due to the complexity of social interactions and experiences, to develop a sound knowledge of other people's strengths and weaknesses, even though credit has all along been given to mutual understanding and inter-subjective social communication. This is compatible with self-defense, self-concealment, and so forth. At the same time, it is more difficult to know and identify one's own demerits or shortcomings, for almost everyone tends to be self-centered and self-opinionated. One is apt to justify and glorify his words and deeds, and so self-criticism and self-knowledge are both recommended and encouraged as twin ideals for personal cultivation and self-development.

The catchphrase 'the most precious of all human qualities is genuine self-knowledge' *(ren gui you zi zhi zhi ming)* is widely appreciated among the Chinese people. It is originated from the DDJ text and has been internalized in the psychology of Chinese nationals in the main. The attainment of these ideals oriented to individual understanding or self-cultivation is largely determined by the degree of one's adherence to the *Dao* as the fountainhead of wisdom. With enough wisdom of this kind, one can be in a position to recognize one's own weaknesses and thereby bolster one's will to overcome them. It is by virtue of so doing that one grows wise and mighty in the pure senses of these terms.

Noticeably profound and dialectical is Laozi's exposure of the importance of self-knowledge and self-conquest in respect of personal weaknesses. This observation is significant and positive from the viewpoint of either epistemology or individual growth. However, there is always a limit to one's cognitive power in this aspect due to the tendency of self-justification, self-glorification, self-centeredness, and self-defensiveness, as mentioned above. In practice, the so-called wisdom of self-knowledge is mostly grounded on an open and receptive attitude toward relevant criticisms and opinions offered by others.

15.2 (Section 47)

Without going out of the door
  One may know all-under-the-sky.
Without looking through the window
  One may see the *Dao* of Heaven.
The further one goes,
  The less one knows.
Therefore the sage knows without going about,
  Understands without seeing,
  And accomplishes without taking action.

Commentary

In this section Laozi denies the value of practical experience or learning, and recommends a contemplative approach to the true knowledge of all things with reference to the *Dao* of Heaven. However, knowledge as such does not mean an accumulated amount of cognition or information about the phenomenological world. It implies, in fact, the most essential insight into the nature of all things. In short, it refers to true knowledge or genuine wisdom in Laozi's terminology.

For a long time this idea has been conceived as something idealistically false, if not humbug. Yet, with more and more people practicing *qigong* as a form of traditional Chinese breathing exercise with stylized movements for spiritual meditation, and as more of its effects has come to be rediscovered, some scholars have commenced to realize the implications of what Laozi says here. Xu Xihua of Yunnan University has testified to this after having practiced *qigong* for over three years.

What Laozi describes here may remind the reader of the experience of Sakyamuni, the founder of Buddhism, who once sat under a tree in meditation for 49 days and nights. It was on the evening of the last day that he finally gained an insight into truth and causality for over three generations ahead. In other words, he had attained the supreme wisdom or enlightenment necessary for attaining Buddhahood. Since then such notions as 'inner or heavenly enlightenment for attaining Buddhahood' (*hui yan tong* or *tian yan tong*) have come to be used in Buddhism. Correspondingly in early Daoism there are such similar notions as 'understanding without seeing' and 'contemplation in depth'.

15.3 (Section 52)

There was a beginning of the universe,
    Which may be called the mother of the universe.
He who has found the mother
    Thereby understands her sons;
He who has understood the sons
    And still keeps to the mother
    Will be free from danger throughout his life.
Block up the holes;
    Shut up the doors
    And till the end of life there will be no toil.
Open the holes;
    Meddle with affairs;
    And till the end of life there will be no salvation.
Seeing what is small is called enlightenment.
Keeping to weakness is called strength.
Use the light.
Revert to enlightenment.
And thereby avoid danger to one's life—
    This is called practicing the eternal.

Commentary

This section deals with the *Dao* as the mother of the universe or the foundation of all beings. Laozi points out that no one will encounter danger if he follows the principle of the *Dao*, principle that calls for avoiding the search of knowledge, and keeping the eyes closed and the ears blocked. Accordingly, one is warned not to be occupied with any enterprise, but to maintain a weak position for the sake of self-defense.

As a matter of fact, the key idea of this section lies in Laozi's advising people to explore the *Dao* as the origin of all things by penetrating their appearances. This is additionally mirrored in his encouraging people to pursue and perceive the inward instead of the outward, so as to eradicate desire and ambition, and meanwhile to foster inner enlightenment and true wisdom. Only by means of this light of wisdom may one get close to the attainment of the *Dao* and preserve the whole of the real self.

Here it is worth clarifying that Laozi looks down upon knowledge but lauds wisdom as is characterized by simplicity and purity of mind. Thus he believes that it is wise not to have any knowledge or any desire for knowledge since this is detrimental in view of self-preservation. As regards Laozi's proposed approach to wisdom, it seems to be somewhat mysterious and incomprehensible when judged from a normally logical and epistemological perspective. Yet, if one has basically experienced what Chinese *qigong* is all about, as a way of spiritual meditation and mental cultivation, one may well understand the approach after all. This corresponds to the content of the previously discussed section. The principal objective of practicing *qigong* is to reduce all one's desires for external things in a materialistic sense and ambitions for personal achievement in a social sense. In short, *qigong* is aimed at helping one return to the mental state of simplicity, having-no-knowledge and pure-mindedness. Such being the case, you become what you are by achieving your real self. Consequently, you hanker after nothing and accordingly remain undisturbed by nothing. Thus you are always free from cares and worries, anxieties and frustrations, among other negative things. Then you do not see the point of taking any risk or adventure. If you manage to get into this frame of mind, how could it be possible that there would be any danger or harm threatening you?

Some of the terms used in this section are noteworthy, for instance, 'the holes' represent the mouth, ears, eyes, and nostrils, which function as channels for perceiving and conveying knowledge or information. 'The doors' is symbolic of the means for communicating and absorbing knowledge or information. 'The light' stands for the pure experience encountered in the higher stages of *qigong* practice. When one moves into the contemplation in depth one may see a light sparkling in front of one's eyes, which is symbolic of the attainment of true enlightenment by which the mind itself is purified of all desires and wants.

15.4 (Section 56)

He who knows does not speak,
   He who speaks does not know.
He blocks the vent,

Closes the door,
Blunts the sharpness,
Unties the tangles,
Softens the glare,
And mixes with the dust.
This is called Profound Identification.

Therefore people cannot get intimate with him,
    Nor can they estrange themselves from him.
People cannot benefit him,
    Nor can they harm him.
People cannot ennoble him,
    Nor can they debase him.
For this reason he is esteemed by all-under-Heaven.

Commentary

Like Section 52 discussed earlier, this section exposes Laozi's condemnation of pretentious knowledge and preference for genuine wisdom derived from the *Dao*. His advocacy of Profound Identification with the *Dao* can be seen as the highest form of achievement in life, and the essential quality of his ideal personality. This being the case, one is supposed to be broad-minded and selfless enough to treat impartially all things in the world.

The advice to 'block the vent, close the door, blunt the sharpness, untie the tangles, soften the glare and mix with the dust' serves as a workable strategy for self-defense and self-preservation, in chaotic times in particular. This in effect corresponds to the Chinese saying, 'Hide one's capacities and bide one's time' (*tao guang yang hui*). However, if one stays passive all the time, he misses his chance when it comes; then, as it is, the whole strategy will turn out to be in vain. Hence it would be better to look into Laozi's advice both critically and reflectively.

More specifically, by reading between the lines would one be able to uncover such metaphorical implications as follows: 'He blocks the vent,' for instance, suggests that one stays away from the knowledge of the world because it will plunge him into the mire of cares and worries; he 'closes the door' suggests that one shut the door of desires because it is the fountainhead of miseries and sufferings; he 'blunts the sharpness' suggests that one conceal or hide his aggressiveness even though one is competent and talented; he 'unties the tangles' suggests that one manage to free oneself from social entanglements and disturbances; he 'softens the glare' suggests that one be modest by covering up his brightness; and finally, he 'mixes with the dust' suggests that one mingle with the profane world or society. As regards the concept of 'Profound Identification' (*xuan tong*), it refers to the sphere of realizing the *Dao*. It is equivalent in meaning to such terms as 'embracing the One' (*bao yi*) and 'attainment of the One' (*de yi*) used elsewhere in the DDJ.

15.5 (Section 71)

It is best to know that you don't know.
It is an aberration to pretend to know when you don't know.
The sage is free from this aberration
   Because he recognizes it as such.
He can be free from this aberration
   Only when he recognizes it as such.

Commentary

This section chiefly reveals Laozi's recommendation of self-knowledge as a fundamental part of true wisdom. It is fairly common around us that some people pretend to know when they do not really know, and some others tend to scratch the surface and thus get some form of superficial knowledge. Yet, they make a big display of their 'half knowledge and half understanding' *(yi zhi ban jie)*. In striking contrast, the sage or the wise man in the pure senses of these terms maintain a sincere and faithful attitude toward truth and wisdom. They do not rush to make any assertion, but first investigate matters inside out and grasp their respective essences.

With regard to Laozi's stress on the self-consciousness of the 'aberration' concerned, it inevitably reminds us of Confucius' remark on real knowledge, that is, 'To say you know when you know, and to say you do not know when you do not know, that is knowledge' (1983: 65 [II.17]). And elsewhere he exclaims, 'Do I possess knowledge? No, I don't. A rustic put a question to me and my mind was a complete blank. I kept hammering at the two sides of the question until I got everything out of it' (1983: 97 [IX.8]). Socrates once made a similar statement, 'I don't think I know what I myself don't know.' And he also says, 'I am a bit more intelligent than others simply because I know that I am ignorant. But others don't know that they are ignorant.' It is fascinating to find that these three thinkers in ancient times happened to share more or less the same view of true knowledge or wisdom. We may presume to conclude that if truth is naked, he who genuinely pursues truth ought to be naked as well in respect of his attitude. That is to say, he must develop a sincere and honest attitude by ridding himself of all fallacies and follies, pretensions and guises. Otherwise, the more he strives for truth, the further will he deviate from it. This principle is figuratively described by the old Chinese saying, 'Trying to go south by driving the chariot north' (*nan yuan bei zhe*), similar in meaning to acting in a way that defeats the purpose.

Chapter 16

On Fortune and Misfortune

Good fortune or happiness is what people hanker after. At the same time, misfortune or misery is what people try to avoid. However, they go hand in hand as though in a kind of twinship. Being two opposites in unity, they are mutually interdependent and transformational. This emerges in Laozi's dialectical thinking as expressed in Section 58 (DDJ).

16.1 (Section 58)

When the government is generous and non-discriminatory,
  The people will remain honest and sincere;
When the government is severe and discriminatory,
  The people will become crafty and cunning.
Misfortune is that beside which fortune lies;
  Fortune is that beneath which misfortune lurks.
Who knows what may be their ultimate cause?
There is no fixed and normal frame of reference.
The normal can suddenly turn into the abnormal.
The good can suddenly turn into the evil.
The people have been deluded for a long time.

Therefore, the sage is as pointed as a square, but never stays stiff;
He is as sharp as a knife, but never cuts anybody;
He is frank and straightforward, but never aggressive;
He is bright and shining, but never dazzling.

Commentary

As has been detected in Laozi's political philosophy, the more severe political control is, the more resistance there arises from the people; and the more generous state government is, the less resistance there arises from the people.

Such evidence is easily available in the human history to prove that whenever and wherever a government strives to set up more rules and regulations to control and punish the people, the people will in turn seek all possible means to shake them off or run away from them. The situation is somewhat like what Wang Bi describes: 'The more sophisticated and elaborate the system of control is schemed, the more adaptable and changeable will the wiles of the people become; the harder the punishment comes, the quicker will the people flee' (Beida, 1980: 253). That is why Laozi advises a government to be generous and non-discriminating instead of being severe and discriminating in order to retain the people plain and simple. In a word, he expects a government not to keep disturbing the people, but to let them enjoy peace and tranquility. The expectation itself naturally developed from his social ideal of bringing order to the chaotic society of his time.

The dialectical thinking of Laozi is further reflected in his exposition of the interactions between fortune and misfortune, normal and abnormal, good and evil. The notion that 'Misfortune is that beside which fortune lies; fortune is that beneath which misfortune lurks' is reminiscent of a parable in *The Book of Huannanzi* which may be fully cited here: There lived an old man near China's northern borders, whose horse by chance wandered into the territory of the northern tribes. All his neighbors commiserated with him over the loss. 'Perhaps this will turn out to be a blessing,' said the old man. After a few months, the horse came back accompanied by another fine horse from the north. Seeing this, all his neighbors congratulated him. 'Perhaps this will turn out to be a cause of misfortune,' said the old man. He prospered and had many fine horses. One day his son, who was fond of riding, fell from a horse and broke his leg. All the neighbors came to commiserate with the family. 'Perhaps this will turn out to be a blessing,' said the old man. One year later, the northern tribes mounted an invasion of the border regions. All able-bodied young men were enlisted to fight against the invaders except for the old man's son, because he was a cripple, and so the old man and his son survived the consequent slaughter (Gao, 1986: 310–11). The lesson of this kind is to testify that an apparent blessing is often misfortune in disguise, and vice versa. For things are bound to change for better or worse under certain conditions.

Then, what should be done about it? According to Laozi, one should not fix his eyes on the positive aspects of things. Instead, he should see through the surface and keep alert against their potentially negative aspects. As a rule, he should manage to stop at the right time and place in what he does in order to keep things from reversing to their opposites.

As regards the interrelationship between misfortune and fortune, Han Feizi argues: 'When a person encounters with misfortune, he will feel fearful; when he feels fearful, he will act uprightly; when he acts uprightly, he will think prudently. At this stage; he will get hold of the principle of things, and be free from misfortune and harm. When he is free from misfortune and harm, he will live his natural term; when he lives his natural term, he will become fulfilled himself and enjoy longevity; when he gets hold of the principle of things, he will be sure to succeed; when he is sure to succeed, he will live a good and dignified life. When he has become fulfilled himself and lived a good and dignified life, he has attained fortune in the pure sense of this term. Hence it is said that 'Misfortune is that beside which fortune lies,' because it helps facilitate the success. Contrarily and reversely, when a person has attained fortune, he will secure an easy access to wealth and nobility; when he has access to wealth and nobility, he will delight himself in beautiful dress and delicious food; when he delights himself in beautiful dress and delicious food, he will grow arrogant; when he is arrogant, he will behave badly and abandon the principle of things. Consequently, he will lose his body and have no chance to succeed. When internally he is in danger to lose his body and externally he has no chance to succeed, he will confront with big misfortune that is actually originated from fortune. Therefore, it is said that 'Fortune is that beneath which misfortune lurks' (1984: 1254).

All in all, Laozi's contribution to dialectical speculation is embodied in his discovery that everything has two sides including fortune and misfortune, normal and abnormal, good and evil, among others. When these two sides develop to a certain point, they will turn into their opposites. This corresponds to the old saying that 'things are sure to return to their opposites when they go to extremes' (*wu ji bi fan*). However, the whole idea as such features some grave drawbacks as follows: First, Laozi realizes the fact that all opposites are mutually interdependent and transformational in view of the law of opposites in unity. Yet, he fails to see the dynamic interaction between each pair of opposites. When acknowledging that everything in the universe is always on the move, he maintains that the movement or change go around in a perpetual circle instead of in a linear progression. Secondly, with respect to movement and tranquility as two important categories in Chinese philosophy, Laozi assumes that tranquility is more essential and decisive than movement as is implied in his statement, 'Though all things flourish with a myriad of variations, each one eventually returns to its root. This return to the root is called tranquility' (DDJ, Sect. 16). The 'root' here means the *Dao* as the origin of all things. His preference for tranquility is compatible with his philosophy of keeping to the tranquil as a whole (DDJ, Sects. 26 and 60). Thirdly, opposites can only be transformed into one another under certain conditions. Otherwise, they will still remain what they are. This is the same with fortune and misfortune. Nevertheless, Laozi absolutizes the transformation by advocating a kind of wait-for-your-turn attitude, as if initiative or subjective endeavor is dispensable and unnecessary. This seems to be misleading, because in practice mutual transformation of that kind can never occur automatically. This shows that his dialectics is incomplete, simplistic and somewhat naive (Fung, 1992: 39–42).

As for Laozi's claim that 'The people have been deluded for a long time,' it basically means that the people tend to follow the beaten track to care about what fortune and misfortune could bring about to them. In most cases, they try every means to avoid any form of misfortune because they think it detrimental to their hopes and expectations for a good life, while striving for the benefits and promises of fortune upon which they think a good life will depend. Laozi attempts here to remind them of the hard fact that misfortune and fortune take up a dialectical interlink. They therefore need to break with the stereotyped psychology of self-preservation, the conventional pursuit of self-interests, the patternized guidance of social ideology, and the shallow cognition of fortune and misfortune. It is for this reason why Laozi recommends the *Dao* of the sage to be followed due to the special virtues as are depicted thereafter.

Chapter 17

On Life and Death

Life and death are crucial issues with which all human beings are deeply concerned. Almost all philosophers, East and West, were and are preoccupied one way or another with varied conceptions of life and death. Laozi attempts to assert that both life and death are as natural as anything else in the world. Zhuangzi, who inherits this line of thought, thinks that they are neither to be welcomed nor rejected. Therefore, these two thinkers in early Daoism advise people to view life and death as nothing but natural phenomena to the extent that the former is not to be overvalued and the latter not to be scared. The best way to preserve life is, according to Laozi, to live out one's own natural term free from cares and worries. This could be possible only when one sees through the value of life and the nature of death. Let us look at Section 50 (DDJ) with reference to some relevant observations given by Zhuangzi.

17.1 (Section 50)

Man comes alive into the world
   And goes dead into the earth.
Three out of ten will live longer.
Three out of ten will live shorter.
And three out of ten will strive for long life
   But meet premature death.
And for what reason?
It is because of excessive preservation of life.
Only those who don't value their lives are wiser
Than those who overvalue their lives.

I have heard that those who are good at preserving life
   Will not meet rhinoceroses or tigers when traveling the byways,
   And will not be wounded or killed when fighting battles.
The rhinoceroses cannot butt their horns against them.
The tigers cannot fasten their claws upon them.

And weapons cannot thrust their blades into them.
And for what reason?
Because they are out of the range of death

Commentary

This section expounds Laozi's attitude toward life and death, which he regards as natural phenomena from his Daoist perspective. The implicit criticism of the rich and powerful, who were obsessed with material enjoyments, reflects Laozi's indignation of the social reality of his age. The 'excessive preservation of life' that is liable to result in premature death comes about through exposure to the destructive effects of the 'five colors' that cause blindness, the 'five tones' that cause deafness, the 'five flavors' that cause the loss of taste, and 'racing and hunting' that cause madness (see 10.1). Observant and critical as he was, Laozi could do nothing to change the situation. He therefore sticks to his philosophy of plainness and simplicity by advising people in general to learn how to preserve life according to the principle of the *Dao*. Under such circumstances, a practical approach lies in belittling the value of life or clinging less tightly to life-consciousness, since only by so doing could one be 'out of the range of death'.

In Zhuangzi's philosophy there is frequent explication of the naturalness of both life and death. Once he even goes so far as to claim that life is like a tumor, and death is taken as the bursting of the tumor. He also contends that all living beings in the world evolve from *qi* as vital energy. Thus one comes to be alive when this vital energy gathers together, and dies when this vital energy disperses. He then describes the stages of human existence as follows: A man toils throughout his life; he lives an easy life when old and retired; and he finally enjoys rest after death. Describing life and death in such a circle, Zhuangzi tells people not to welcome life when it turns up, and not to resist death when it comes along. He himself is alleged to beaten a drum while singing on the occasion of the natural death of his beloved wife.

According to early Daoism, one can achieve freedom in the pure sense of the word only when he sees through the character of death as a natural phenomenon or an inevitable end. This argument is of course open to criticism and reflection as well, for it is somewhat shrouded in a paradox. In one sense, it could be conceived as something pessimistic and negative. One might be crushed down by such an attitude toward death, and thereby reduce himself to a passive being due to the inevitability of death. In other words, he would set no aims but muddle through life simply because death is like a sword hanging overhead, ready to fall at any minute. He would have no drive for any higher achievement of which man as man is capable, but wait for the coming of death instead. This being the case, whether to be or not to be is no longer a question, simply because this kind of living (life) is not distinct from non-living (death). All this reminds us of the Chinese saying, 'Nothing is more sorrowful than the death of heart [i.e. loss of hope]' (*ai da mo guo yu xin si*).

In the other sense, this view of death can also result in a positive attitude toward life. Since one is highly aware of the inevitability of death, he may attach a value to life. Thus he may make the most of his life because life means everything to himself in spite of its being short. He would be conscious of time that flies and never repeats itself. Accordingly, 'he who has high aspirations tends to sigh over the quick passage of each day.' He will try to grasp every second and work hard. Consequently he will contribute more in his lifetime, expecting his achievement to extend the duration of his existence into the continuing course of human enterprise as a whole.

Moreover, he who accepts death as much a natural phenomenon as life will be able to make light of whatever hardships, difficulties, miseries and sufferings encountered. He may possibly devote his life to a greater cause for the common good of humankind, or choose to die a heroic death for his ideals, for instance. Confucianism recommends that a gentleman should give up his body for the sake of humanity. This spirit obviously demands a positive sense of death as it is regarded as a way of becoming immortal.

To mention in passing, 'Three out of ten will live longer' is the English rendering of the original expression *shi you san* that appears somewhat ambiguous. Han Feizi assumes that it refers to the four limbs and the nine cavities including the ears, eyes, nostrils, mouth, tongue and throat. Wang Bi interprets it as 'three out of ten'. Yang Xingshun reckons that life followed by death in a cycle is one of the natural laws radiating from the *Dao*. Thus, he translates it as 'a third' (of all the people in human society). Like some Laozi scholars, Chen Guying adopts Wang Bi's and Yang Xingshun's interpretations, and affirms that the total of all human beings consists of those (three out of ten) who will live longer, those (three out of ten) who will live shorter, those (three out of ten) who will strive for long life but meet premature death, and those (one out of ten) who are good at preserving life and enjoy longevity (Chen, 1992: 258–9). I accept Chen's interpretation in this context.

Chapter 18

On the Merits of Contentment

A saying widespread among the Chinese people goes: 'He who is contented [with what he has] is always merry and happy' (*zhi zu zhe chang le*). This notion is in fact derived from Laozi's view on the causes of social ills in his days. His recommendation of contentment, or self-contentment, if properly perceived, still has certain import in tackling the problems with the commodity society today. The focus of the discussion falls on Sections 44 and 46 (DDJ).

18.1 (Section 44)

Which is more dear, fame or life?
Which is more valuable, life or wealth?
Which is more detrimental, gain or loss?
Thus an excessive love of fame
   Is bound to cause an extravagant expense.
A rich hoard of wealth
   Is bound to suffer a heavy loss.
Therefore he who is contented will encounter no disgrace.
He who knows when and where to stop will meet no danger.
And in this way he can endure longer.

Commentary

Hereby Laozi advises people to value and treasure life instead of fame and wealth. He sees the latter as causes of danger in one sense, and in another sense as something that can be gained but never maintained, for they are external things (*wai wu*) and not beneficial to life at all. In human society as a whole, what the common folks desire and pursue are chiefly fame and wealth. They may go so far as to be enslaved by 'the reins of fame and the shackles of wealth' (*ming njiang li suo*) as metaphorically depicted in one of the Chinese old sayings.

   As a result, Laozi recommends the merit of being contented with what one has. By virtue of self-contentment one can be free from disgrace and danger, and endure longer. This idea seems to be an extension of that 'he who is contended is rich' as is stated in Section 33 (DDJ, see 15.1).

As regards his preference for life, Laozi does not necessarily expect any excessive preservation of it. He rounds out the value of life in contrast with fame and wealth. The implied message in this context turns out to be a warning to the greed-ridden rich and fame-thirsty people. In respect of the emphasis on self-contentment, Laozi preaches the notion that the more easily one is contented with what one has, the closer will he get to the principle of the *Dao*. In other words, one is most apt to live a more tranquil and peaceful life embellished with rich spiritual nourishment if he is contented with whatever material possessions he has. Nevertheless, a distorted interpretation of self-contentedness would be rather misleading for it may seduce a person into justifying his passivity, laziness and even parasitism.

18.2 (Section 46)

When the world has the *Dao*,
  Warhorses are used in farming.
When the world lacks the *Dao*,
  Even mares in foal have to serve in battle.
There is no guilt greater than lavish desires.
There is no calamity greater than discontentment.
There is no defect greater than covetousness.
Therefore, he who is contented with knowing contentment
  Is always contented indeed.

Commentary

All wars and social conflicts are, in Laozi's observation, unexceptionally ascribed to lavish desires, discontentment, greed, or ambition. He persistently opposes warfare. Thus he repeatedly advocates the importance of acting upon the principle of the *Dao* and meanwhile protests against any resorting to military action at the expense of political stability and social order.

Interestingly, his sharp criticism of discontentment underlines the necessity and significance of contentment. The statement that 'he who is contented with knowing contentment is always contented' can be understood as a high dimension in Laozi's doctrine of self-contentment. It seems to be an initial contentment when one is contended with what he has. For such contentment is based on material possessions after all. Then it seems to be a sublimated contentment when one is contented with knowing contentment. For such contentment at the second stage is fulfilled by spiritual satisfaction in principle. As a rule, it is through the former that the latter is possible as a consequence of a higher sphere of personal cultivation.

Chapter 19

On the Possibilities of Achievement

Laozi is often misunderstood as an advocate of 'doing nothing' or 'non-action,' through which one is expected to abstain from society or reject any social commitment. The fact of the matter is that Laozi keeps advising people to take no arbitrary action, follow the way of spontaneity, and act for others but not compete with them. A close reading of Sections 63 and 64 (DDJ) will help one recognize the true meaning of 'take-no-action' (*wu wei*).

19.1 (Section 63)

Consider take-no-action as a code of conduct.
Consider make-no-trouble as a way of deed.
Consider have-no-flavor as a method of taste.

It is a rule in the world that
   The most difficult things begin with the easy ones,
   And the largest things arise from the minute ones.
Hence, tackle the difficult while it is still easy;
   Achieve the large while it is still minute.
For this reason, the sage never strives for the great,
   And thereby he can accomplish it.

He who makes promises too readily will surely lack credibility.
He who takes things too easily will surely encounter difficulties.
Therefore, even the sage regards things as difficult,
   And he is free from difficulties as a result.

Commentary

The first three lines in this section are in fact stating three principles of human conduct in accordance with the characteristics of the *Dao* in Laozi's formulation.

In respect of the third principle that is to 'consider have-no-flavor as a method of taste,' it seems to reflect the idea presented in Section 35 that 'The *Dao*, if spoken out, is insipid and tasteless' (*Dao zhi chu kou, dan hu qi wu wei*).

The main theme of this section is concerned with the strategies of handling difficult matters on the one hand, and the possibilities of achievement on the other. In the former case, it requires constant prudence and care, apart from an all-round view of things. That is to say, one must see things from both the difficult and easy aspects. Then in the latter case, one should commence with the easy, at the same time as being conscious of taking even the easy as the difficult. Making a great achievement involves a dialectical insight into the process of the inherent progression from the small to the great. Hence, one must remain modest and persevering, and adopt a step-by-step or bit-by-bit policy. One should begin with the small, which then rolls and gathers matter like a snowball pushed forward with continuous efforts.

In brief, practical wisdom in Daoism works to expose and reinforce the notion that the great develops from the small, and the many from the few. All this reveals Laozi's sharp observation of the inner development of things in general and their dynamic transformation in particular. He therefore concludes, 'It is a rule in the world that the most difficult things begin with the easy ones, and the largest things arise from the minute ones.'

What else is noteworthy is the observation that 'He who makes promises too readily will surely lack credibility.' From antiquity up till now, it is always considered virtuous to keep promise. As is acknowledged, the superior man (*jun zi*) takes it a most serious matter to have word of honor. It is therefore announced that a four-horse chariot cannot run fast enough to catch up with the word uttered. This means when a promise is made, it must be kept and implemented instead of being forgotten or cast aside, because it reflects one's personality apart from his honesty and trustworthiness. For this reason, one must think prudently and make promises seriously as it is by no means a simple craft of rhetoric. If one makes promises without due consideration, he is apt in most cases to take them so lightly, and even shelf them up soon afterwards. He is therefore criticized and warned by Laozi at this point.

19.2 (Section 64)

What is stable is easy to hold.
What is not yet manifest is easy to handle.
What is brittle is easy to disintegrate.
What is minute is easy to eliminate.
Deal with matters before they occur.
Put them in order before disorder arises.
A tree as huge as one's embrace grows from a tiny shoot.
A tower of nine stories rises from a heap of earth.

A journey of a thousand miles starts from the first step.
People often fail when they are on the point of success
    In their conduct of affairs.
If they remain still as careful at the end as at the beginning,
    They will never suffer failures.

Commentary

This section attempts to illustrate through specific examples the interrelationship or interaction between the big and the small, the high and the low, and the long and the short. It also advises people to cultivate a spirit of both persistency and patience in pursuit of their targets. In addition, it encourages people to become more prudent and cautious when they are approaching the end of any task. Otherwise they are most likely to ruin the whole business when they are right on the threshold of success.

Experience teaches that identifying the cause of a potential catastrophe enables measures to be taken to prevent it. That is why we have such sayings springing from the collective wisdom as follows: 'Prevention is better than cure,' and 'take an umbrella with you when there is a sign of rain.'

It is equally important to take into account the potential change and development of things encountered. According to Laozi, the great develops from the small, the high from the low, and the long from the short. During this process, one must take relevant and precautionary steps so as to bring things under control. It is therefore advisable to tackle a problem 'in the cradle' so to speak, otherwise it will grow to an unmanageable size and eventually turn into its opposite. A dam of a thousand miles long, for instance, may be destroyed as a result of an ant boring a hole in it. Likewise, a building of 10,000 feet high may be destroyed by a single spark. These two parabolic cases are popular among the Chinese people and often cited to justify the above-mentioned argument. Accordingly, he who is regarded as wise is a man observant enough to pinpoint the problem at the very beginning, and then is ready to cope with it at the earliest possible moment.

In view of Laozi's warning that 'People often fail when they are about to succeed in their conduct of affairs,' we may arrive at the conclusion that whatever one tries to do, one will be rebuffed in the end if one lacks prudence and perseverance. It is noticeable in everyday life that most people tend to be over-pleased with preliminary success or minor gains at the first stages of their endeavors. Thus they overlook the hard reality that 'He who laughs last laughs best.' Others (especially opponents or enemies) are eager to take advantage of such carelessness to the extent of setting a trap by dangling bait first, and then knocking the victim down with a club when he takes it (see 20.4).

Chapter 20

On the Art of Leadership

Laozi's political philosophy is amply reflected in his discussion of the art of leadership. It features 'take-no-action,' 'non-competition,' 'retreat for the sake of advance,' 'keep to the tender,' and so forth. Driven or stimulated by their personal experiences and practical demands, many DDJ readers project their own ideas or read modern themes into the book. That is why it is continually read and reread and new discoveries are constantly surfacing. Scrutiny of the following 11 Sections (DDJ) will illustrate this.

20.1 (Section 3)

Try not to exalt the worthy
   So that the people shall not compete.
Try not to value rare treasures,
   So that the people shall not steal.
Try not to display the desirable,
   So that the people's hearts shall not be disturbed.
Therefore the sage governs the people by
   Purifying their minds,
   Filling their bellies,
   Weakening their ambitions,
   And strengthening their bones.
He always keeps them innocent of knowledge and desires,
   And makes the crafty afraid to run risks.
He conducts affairs on the principle of take-no-action,
   And everything will surely fall into order.

Commentary

This section has long been interpreted as an art of leadership. It advises the ruling class not to elevate the worthy, not to value rare treasures and not to display or show off the desirable, so that the human competitive instinct may be diminished. This is precisely because competition among people tends to stir up social confusion and chaos.

On the other hand, it advises the ruler to learn the art of governance from the sage. That is to follow the given strategies as such: (1) To purify their minds (*xu qi xin*). It suggests keeping their minds vacuous and free from all greedy ideas or competitive intentions. The Chinese term *xu* literally means 'empty,' which implies here absolute peace and purity of mind, and freedom from worry and selfish desires (Chan, 1973: 141). (2) To fill their bellies (*shi qi fu*). It literally denotes the satisfaction of people's basic needs, such as their physical needs for food and drink. The implied message is related to the possibility of easy contentment with what one has in contrast to insatiable greed stimulated by external things (i.e. wealth and fame). This expression should be read with particular reference to Laozi's phrase in Section 12, 'The sage therefore cares for the belly instead of the eyes' (see 10.1). In fact, deeply rooted in the Chinese way of thinking is the notion that 'people give the food supply priority,' and this has had a chronic influence on governmental policies from ancient times until today. One of its negative aspects can be seen in the conventional overemphasis on food or eating in daily life and at festivals as well. The Chinese people tend to consider a festival a special occasion for a big feast. Although the modern trend is to frown on the traditional extravagance displayed at feasts, such celebrations can be regarded as a distinct cultural phenomenon with its own special features, say, the rich variety of cuisine and the enjoyment of a harmonious ambiance. (3) To weaken their ambitions (*ruo qi zhi*). It means to reduce people's desire or impulse for competition: The petty man (*xiao ren*) gets up early in the morning to pursue profit, and the superior man (*jun zi*) does the same in order to promote his reputation and standing. They act so because they are motivated only by their ambitions. This kind of obsession will at the very least heat up the competition in society and bring about disorder. Moreover, it will result in the loss of one's real self owing to the fact that one constantly fall a victim to alienation and enslavement by either one's ambitions or desires. In addition, it stirs up the tendency of people to play tricks upon each other. (4) To strengthen their bones (*qiang qi gu*). It literally means to make people healthy and strong. It might also imply making them satisfied and contented by doing so. When these four strategies are successfully carried out, the people are most prone to become 'innocent of knowledge and desires' (*wu zhi wu yu*). At his stage they may have no much knowledge of how to resort to crafty ideas in order to win the upper hand, and have no more desires to compete or struggle for more gains.

In ancient Chinese thought, the ruler is often likened to a boat and the people to water. The boat can sail smoothly when the water is calm, whereas it can be turned over when the water swirls in anger. This analogy illustrates vividly the interaction between the ruling class and the ordinary people. It thus attempts to warn the ruling class that they cannot afford to ignore their subjects in general, and their fundamental needs in particular. Otherwise, the tables will be bound to turn in their disfavor. Such being the case, we can better understand what was said by Mao Zedong when he led the Red Army to have arrived in Yanan in 1935: The masses are ready to hanker after social reform and to stir up political revolution when they are poverty-stricken. This implies that as human beings all work and struggle to survive, they may have no other choice but to rise in revolt if their subsistence is threatened. This does not necessarily mean that all humans are the same, for it is granted that some people live for ideals rather than for making their ends meet or filling their bellies.

'He conducts affairs on the principle of take-no-action.' This is a notion running throughout Laozi's ideology. It calls up a ruler to do things or conduct state affairs in the most natural way possible, without being arbitrary and high-handed in ruling his subjects. Accordingly, it must be pointed out that the notion of being 'without knowledge' is conceived by some Laozi scholars as something to do with making people ignorant and stupid. It actually means reducing people's motives to play tricks or engage in craftiness in the competition involved in human activities. Correspondingly, the expression 'without desires' is employed to mean that instinctive desire is to be conserved, while greedy or social desire for material possessions is to be eschewed since it is a crucial cause of all the problems arising in human society.

The expression of 'exalt the worthy' (*shang xian*) seems not simply to be a strategy utilized by a ruler to attract the worthy, but also a way of attaining a good name for himself. Throughout the course of Chinese history, there are many examples of rulers who made good use of men who were qualified or worthy for social accomplishments, even though they often promoted to high positions some others who were mere frauds.

The development of material civilization is prone to foster and reinforce people's desires for possessions. A close observation of modern advertising bears this out. It thus reduces people to the plight of being passive consumers or slaves of commodities. A considerable proportion of human anxiety, frustration, and depression, which together comprise psycho-cultural problems, can be perceived as a consequence of the commercial display of desirable things. If by any chance all the mass media ceased to display such things, I assume that tension, either in a social or psychological sense, may well be relaxed to a great extent. If we approach Laozi's thought from this perspective in relation to the present human condition, we are most likely to rediscover new and rich implications in his canons. This explains why his book, short as it is in a length of 5000 words or so, can be read and re-read, continually revealing fresh messages and enlightenment.

20.2 (Section 26)

The heavy is the root of the light.
The tranquil is the lord of the hasty.

Therefore the sage travels all day
   Without leaving behind his baggage cart.
Although he enjoys a magnificent and comfortable life,
   He remains at leisure and without self-indulgence in it.
How is it that a king with ten thousand chariots
   Governs his kingdom so lightly and hastily?
Lightness is sure to lose the root.
Hastiness is sure to lose the lord.

Commentary

In ancient times 'the heavy' and 'the light' were referred to two types of chariot. When engaged in a military action, the light chariots were usually used to attack the enemy on the frontline, while the heavy chariot used to support the action as they carried the relevant supplies, provisions and other necessities. It is in a practical sense that the heavy chariots are considered to be the root or foundation of the light chariots (Gu and Guan, 2009: 286–7).

In this context, the heavy and the light are metaphorically employed to symbolize two methods of conducting state affairs. That is to say, the heavy is compared to the ruler whereas the light to the courtiers and subjects all together. The ruler is advised to keep power for governance and administration under his control even when his subordinates are sent around to handle different kinds of tasks. In this aspect, the ruler seems to work as the mind, and the subordinates as the limbs. In addition, the heavy is also conceived to mean the stable and prudent way of governance while the light the unstable and imprudent way of governance. When the former strategy is applied, the power structure and social stability will be secured. If by any chance the latter is applied, it will give rise to political disorder and social chaos.

In respect to 'the tranquil' and 'the hasty,' they are allegorical to two opposite approaches to governance: one is reasonably cool-minded and carefully observant while the other rather rush and harsh in both making decisions and conducting state affairs. The contradictions between them are ostensible. With the former favored and the latter rejected, Laozi persistently advises the ruler to adopt his political philosophy of 'take-no-(arbitrary)-action,' which he thinks is the general principle of competent and good governance.

In reality the ruler functions as the hub of a state or governmental machine. Hence what he does will naturally affect the entire operation of the machine. If he governs his kingdom lightly and hastily, in Laozi's terms, the ruler will plunge not only himself but also the whole country into trouble or chaos. It is for this reason that he is recommended to be prudent and play safe in respect of his political policy and governmental administration.

20.3 (Section 36)

In order to contract it,
   It is necessary to expand it first.
In order to weaken it,
   It is necessary to strengthen it first.
In order to destroy it,
   It is necessary to promote it first.
In order to grasp it,
   It is necessary to offer it first.
This is called subtle light.

The soft and the tender overcome the hard and the strong.
(Just as) fish should not be taken away from deep water,
   The sharp weapons of the state should not be displayed to the people.

Commentary

The key concept in this section is 'subtle light' as a literal rendering of the original expression *wei ming*, which figuratively means 'profound and predictive insight into what is going to take place the other way round.' It is conceptually illustrated and justified by the subsequent line: 'The soft and the tender overcome the hard and the strong.' Some Laozi scholars assume that 'subtle light' indicates a natural law of change appearing shrouded in obscurity but remaining manifest in reality.

Laozi consistently holds on to his observation that everything has two sides in a state of continuous opposition and mutual transformation. That is to say, when one of the two sides develops to its acme, it will inevitably be transformed into its opposite. This dialectical thought is reflected in his description of the interrelations and interactions between contraction and expansion, weakening and strengthening, and destruction and promotion, as well as grasping and giving. His analysis of the development of these matters and phenomena naturally leads to his generalization that 'Reversion is the movement of the *Dao*' presented in Section 40 (DDJ).

A flower, for example, will naturally wither or close up (contraction) when it is in full bloom (expansion). Thus the latter can be viewed as a sign of the former state. Conversely, an inchworm draws itself together when it wants to stretch out. Dragons and snakes hibernate in order to preserve their lives and activities. It is therefore concluded that 'contraction and expansion impel each other on, and benefits are generated in this process' (Lynn, 1994: 31).

As regards this dialectical thought of Laozi, it seems what Laozi argues in this context concerns about the natural development of things that is beyond human perception in general. All things in the world are sure to reverse themselves when they reach their extremes. The sun will, for instance, start to descend and set in the west when it is overhead shining to its fullest; the moon will begin to wane as soon as it is completely full. So natural is the movement of things. Expansion is therefore a sign of the imminence of contraction; the strong is therefore the sprouting of the weak; the flourishing is therefore a harbinger of the declining; the given is therefore a symptom of the taken. Both natural phenomena and human affairs develop and change in such a natural and inevitable way. Ordinary people who encounter these things are unable to predict or recognize what is behind them. It is for this reason that the *Dao* is called the 'subtle light.'

It is noteworthy that these lines are often misconceived and misinterpreted as conspiratorial tactics applied to power-games. And accordingly, Laozi himself is often labeled a political conspirator. This is understandable to the extent that each DDJ reader is liable to form one's own image of Laozi by reading personal or modern ideas and feelings into his book. It is no wonder that there are, as the saying goes, as many types of Hamlet as there are audiences. The same is also true of Laozi. We tend to maintain that Laozi describes the interactions between all those categories simply in order to justify his conception of the inexorable transformation between opposites.

According to Gao Heng, Laozi is here talking about the *Dao* of Heaven or the natural law. Hence it is groundless to accuse him of being a conspirator (Gao, 1988: 81). As can be noticed throughout DDJ, Laozi often exposes his theses first, and then leaves off by warning the ruling class of what they should not do. This section is no exception. That 'the sharp weapons of the state should not be displayed to the people' is intended to advise the rulers not to apply severe laws, orders and regulations when controlling, punishing, or threatening the people. This may bring about more trouble than benefit because when driven into a corner the people will rise in revolt against 'the sharp weapons of the state' and the ruling class which wields them. These 'weapons' are in fact symbolic of the strong that cannot last long since they are, in Laozi's terms, the companions of death.

20.4 (Section 59)

To rule people and to serve Heaven
    Nothing is better than the principle of frugality.
Only by frugality can one get ready early.
To get ready early means to accumulate the *De* continuously.
With the continuous accumulation of the *De*,
    One can overcome every difficulty.
If one can overcome every difficulty,
    He will then acquire immeasurable capacity.
With immeasurable capacity,

He can achieve the *Dao* to govern the country.
He who has the *Dao* of the country can maintain sovereignty.
This is called the way in which the roots are planted deep,
    And the stalks are made firm;
    Longevity is achieved,
    And sovereignty is made everlasting.

Commentary

Laozi recommends in this section 'the principle of frugality' in a spiritual rather than material sense. He warns the ruling class not to display 'the sharp weapons of the state' frequently or use them indiscreetly, otherwise disorder and revolt may result. Meanwhile he advises people not to do what they should not do; instead they should preserve their energy and nourish their spirit by reducing acquisitive desires and arbitrary actions. As a strategy, frugality is conducive to longevity and the maintenance of sovereignty.

20.5 (Section 60)

Governing a large country is like cooking a small fish.
If the *Dao* is applied to the world,
    Ghosts will lose their supernatural influence.
It is not that they will actually lose it,
    But that their influence will no longer be able to harm men.
It is not that their influence will no longer be able to harm men,
    But that the sage also will not harm men.
Since these two do not harm men, and vice versa,
    They all enjoy peaceful co-existence.

Commentary

The idea of 'governing a large country is like cooking a small fish' has become a well-known aphorism in political praxis. It is often taken as a strategy for conducting state affairs, widely noted for its long, historical, and even international influence. Former US President Ronald Reagan, for instance, once cited this line in one of his public speeches according to his understanding of what it is supposed to mean. This event has led to one more English version of DDJ. However, this line does not mean anything easy as regards state administration or governance. Instead, it bears an implicit warning to the ruling class. That is, a small fish can be ruined if it is turned over too often while being cooked, so too can disorder be brought about in a state if the people are disturbed by too many orders and decrees. This being the case, a ruler should become highly conscious that the mystique of or the key to good governance lies in the *Dao* of cherishing tranquility and taking no arbitrary action, for the sake of the public interest and social stability.

In the final analysis, the art of governance as recommended by Laozi is factually an extension of his philosophy of taking no arbitrary action and following the way of spontaneity. He offers advice of this kind not simply as a strategy for the benefit of the ruling class, but also due to his concern about the harsh conditions the ordinary people had to endure at that time.

As can be discerned in this section, Laozi demonstrates his atheist stance in respect of the imagined preternaturalness of ghosts or deities. This argument can be supported in a twofold way. First, these supernatural beings would no longer function if the *Dao* were applied to governing the world. This obviously implies that the *Dao* is more decisive and important in effect. Second, the practitioners of the *Dao* are certainly human beings. They can maintain their own dignity in the face of supernatural beings. The implications of this kind have such a historical significance that Xunzi reaches the conclusion that 'Man is bound to conquer Heaven.'

It can be also observed by reading between the lines that Laozi intends to tell the reader in a roundabout way that disasters or scourges are caused by men themselves, and not other beings. If men act upon the *Dao* as they ought to, they will remain free from any danger or harm which is allegedly emanated from external things. This naturally reminds us of Laozi's persistent opposition to acquisitive desires and competitive drives on the part of human beings.

20.6 (Section 61)

Governing a large country is like lying in a lower place.
This country may be likened to rivers and streams
    Flowing into the sea.
It lies lower such that all in the world runs to it.
It is the converging point of all in the world.
It is the female of the world
    That always overcomes the male via tranquility
    And with tranquility she lies lower.
Hence a big state can rally small states around it
    If it lowers itself to them.
Small states can win trust from a big state
    If they lower themselves to it.
Thus a big state can rally small states by lowering itself.
Small states can win trust from a big state by lowering themselves.
What a big state wants is to unite and lead small states.

What small states want is to be rallied and protected by the big state.
When both sides get what they respectively want,
The big state should learn to keep itself lower.

Commentary

This section is apparently reveals Laozi's expounding on his political philosophy. It is chiefly about how to develop and maintain good relationships between large and small states. His notion of being friendly and modest by 'lying in a lower place' is highly advisable to large and powerful countries even today. Only by doing so can they win the trust of small states and contribute to stability and peace. The current policy of peaceful co-existence can be seen as an extension of Laozi's doctrine.

Laozi's political recommendations are based on the historical situation of his time, when China was composed of a group of states of varying sizes, and no longer a unified country. There were constant clashes between the states, among which the larger and stronger would bully the smaller and weaker. The unity of China then was gradually achieved through war annexation. Laozi himself was preoccupied with the attainment and maintenance of peace, but persistently opposed brutal warfare, which only resulted in the suffering of the common people. That is why he advises states, whether large or small, to remain friendly and modest to each other for the sake of mutual trust and acceptability. It must be borne in mind that the large and powerful countries are assumed by Laozi to play the major role in this realm in general.

20.7 (Section 66)

The great rivers and seas can be the kings of the mountain streams
    Because they skillfully stay below them.
That is why they can be their kings.
Therefore, in order to be above the people,
    The sage must place himself below them in his words.
In order to be ahead of the people,
    He must place himself behind them in his person.
In this way, the sage is above the people,
    But they do not feel his weight.
He is ahead of the people,
    But they do not feel his hindrance
Therefore the whole world delights in praising him
    And never gets tired of him.
Simply because he does not compete with others,
    Nobody under Heaven can compete with him.

Commentary

In this section Laozi expresses his leadership tactics that feature non-competition and modesty. He advises the ruling class to stay 'below' and 'behind' instead of 'above' and 'ahead' of the ruled so as to win the latter over, just like the great rivers and seas into which all mountain streams run. This is also the way the powerful avoid disturbing or putting too much pressure on the populace. Otherwise the people's lives will become disturbed and spoiled for certain.

Laozi lauds the image of the sage ruler, who is held up as a model simply because he is not at all arrogant in his treatment of people; he does things without competing for personal fame or gain, and he leads the people without threatening them by showing off his power. If he is by any chance so self-centered that he always thinks of his own benefits first and pushes himself ahead of others, he is liable to be detested, and even overthrown by his subordinates or subjects, or both.

20.8 (Section 72)

When people do not fear the power of the ruler,
    Something terribly dreadful will take place.
Do not force the people out of their dwellings.
Do not exploit the people to the point that they cannot live.
They will not detest and overthrow the regime
    Only when they are not excessively oppressed.

Commentary

In the case of governing a country, Laozi strongly opposes all high-handed policies. Thus he warns the ruling class not to push the people to extremes. Otherwise, they will be driven to rebel in desperation.

History provides a wealth of examples showing that the abuse of power or despotism in any conceivable form will eventually lead to self-defeat or self-destruction. The relationship between the government and the people is allegorically identical to the interaction between a boat and the water. The water below not only sustains the boat as it flows on the surface, it can also capsize it if the waves are stirred up in anger.

20.9 (Section 73)

He who is brave in daring will be killed.
He who is brave in not daring will survive.

Of these two kinds of bravery,
   One is advantageous, while the other is harmful.
Heaven detests what it detests.
Who knows its cause?
The *Dao* of Heaven does not compete, and yet it is good at winning.
It does not speak, and yet it is good at responding.
It is not called, and yet it comes along on its own.
It is frankly at ease, and yet it plans well.
The net of Heaven is large and vast,
   It lets nothing escape, despite its wide meshes.

Commentary

The meaning of the first line can be completed by expanding it to 'He who is brave in daring to be hard and stiff will perish.' This is an extension of the idea that 'The hard and stiff are the companions of death.' Then, the idea embedded in the second line can be completed by expanding it to 'He who is brave in not daring to be hard and stiff but in being tender and weak will survive.' This obviously includes the notion that 'The tender and weak are the companions of life.' Actually this section lays forth 'Laozi's attitude toward life and the idea of predestination. In his opinion, all things are disposed of by Nature. Man has to put himself at the disposal of nature, striving for nothing, doing nothing, saying nothing, which is all to the good, whereas action brings unfavorable consequences' (Ren, 1993: 94).

It is fairly apparent that Laozi intends to stress only the functions of the natural law while neglecting the initiative of humankind. It is on this point that his argument turns out to be somewhat lop-sided. However, it is deemed that Laozi attempts to distinguish between two kinds of bravery from his Daoist perspective on the one hand, and on the other, from his affirmative stance toward the tender and the weak and his negative one toward the hard and the stiff. For he believes that the *Dao* of Heaven or the natural law as such remains tender, weak and non-competitive, but at the same time it is beneficial and not harmful to anything. It is highly appreciated and recommended, as contrasted with the *Dao* of human, which features how to compete against and outshine others by means of power or strength. By his advocacy of the *Dao* of Heaven Laozi expects people in general to modify their conduct according to the non-competitive principle of the *Dao*, and the ruler in particular to improve his leadership based on the model of the *Dao* of Heaven. In other words, Laozi adivses the ruler to follow the way of spontaneity instead of taking arbitrary and competitive action. Thus the ruler could successfully adhere to the road of the *Dao* of Heaven as described in the following: It 'does not compete, and yet it is good at winning. It does not speak, and yet it is good at responding. It is not called, and yet it comes along on its own. It is frankly at ease, and yet it plans well.' This way would manifest Laozi's political philosophy known as 'governing the country without taking action (*wu wei er zhi*).'

By the way, the metaphysical use of 'the net of Heaven' (*tian wang*) has at least two leading interpretations: one refers to the scope of nature in which all things are included and become what they are. The other refers to the function of the *Dao* of Heaven by which all things are determined or affected in their process of becoming and development. Nowadays, it is often used to mean Heaven as a supreme lord or power that observes all things and all actions. Anyone who commits a crime will be discerned, discovered and punished because he takes a blind, wrong and even evil action.

20.10 (Section 74)

If the people are not afraid of death,
    What is the point of trying to frighten them with death?
In order to make people always afraid of death,
    We can catch and kill the trouble-makers.
Then, who will dare to make trouble?
There is always a master in charge of executions.
To carry out executions in place of the master
    Is like hewing wood in place of a skillful carpenter.
Of those who hew wood in place of the carpenter,
    Very few escape cutting their own hands.

Commentary

This section expresses a very crucial aspect of Laozi's political philosophy. 'If the people are not afraid of death, what is the point of trying to frighten them with death?' This really poses a challenging question. Its relevance today is even significant in most of the countries under the control of dictatorship.

Historically in most times of chaos and disorder, the ruler who tries to stabilize the situation tends to resort to punishment. He therefore catches and kills the so-called 'trouble-makers' or leading rebels in order to frighten other would-be rebels or reactionaries. This corresponds to the old Chinese adage about 'killing the chicken to scare the monkey.' But if the people are not afraid of death, punishment cannot be a deterrent.

Seeing the limited function of execution as a widely applied instrument of political suppression, Laozi warms the ruling class not to go too far. The implied message of the last five lines in this section seems to be that those who carry out such a severe punishment as execution to an excessive degree will only injure themselves in the end. They may be like the skilled carpenter who can never avoid cutting his fingers when hewing wood. Hence leadership in general should be cautious enough not to drive the people into a corner by waving the club. Otherwise the latter are apt to rise in rebellion and overthrow their masters.

Moreover, as regards these lines that 'In order to make people always afraid of death, we can catch and kill the trouble-makers. Then, who will dare to make trouble?,' one will find that Laozi is criticizing those who attempt to keep people in fear by killing the trouble-makers or rebels if he relates it to the whole context concerned. To my understanding, Laozi is trying here to convince the reader that the killer of this type will eventually bring himself to dooms. It is somewhat similar in meaning to another old Chinese saying, that is, 'he who lifts a stone to hit another person will drop it on his toes.' To my mind, Laozi seems to give a warning to the ruling class in this case, asking them not to 'kill a chicken to frighten the monkey' because it will bring harm to themselves in that the people are not afraid of death. If by any chance they are driven into a dead corner, they will take the risk of grouping themselves into an uprising by taking drastic and radical actions.

20.11 (Section 75)

The people suffer from famine
  Because the ruler levies too much tax-grain.
Thus they suffer from famine.
The people are difficult to rule
  Because the ruler too often takes action.
Thus they are difficult to rule.
The people take life lightly
  Because the ruler longs for life so avidly.
Thus they take life lightly.

Commentary

In most of the DDJ versions, this section has one more line, which reads 'Only those who don't value their lives are wiser than those who overvalue their lives.' This has been inserted in Section 50 (DDJ), for it fits the context there, according to the textual and philological studies made by Gu Di (1991: 398; also see Chapter 17 of the present volume).

Generally speaking, this section exposes the interactions between the ruling and the ruled. The latter suffer a lot simply because the former have too much enjoyment. Thus there arise conflicts between the two parties. And accordingly the social order will be at stake. It is due to this potential crisis that Laozi advises the ruling class to be on guard against 'blood-sucking'. They should learn not to abandon themselves to luxury and prolonging their lives. Rather, they ought to care whether or not the ruled will 'take life lightly'. By 'taking life lightly' is meant that the populace are driven by desperation to revolt. At this point real trouble arises, and social chaos emerges.

Chapter 21

On Warfare

The book of Laozi is taken by some people to be one bearing some important military ideas, in spite of the fact that Laozi himself generally maintains an anti-war stance (e.g. Fung, 1992: 37–38). In the military arena, Laozi proposes a defensive policy that is firmly based on his notion of retreat as advance. Developed from this defensive policy are such military strategies and tactics as 'wait at one's ease for an exhausted enemy,' 'defend in order to attack,' and 'retreat in order to advance,' which are all intended to 'gain mastery or win victory by striking only after the enemy has struck.' In addition, Laozi's exposure of the interactions between the 'normal way' (*zheng*) and the 'unusual or extraordinary way' (*qi*) contains a rich dialectical message. Sections 57, 68, and 69 (DDJ) touch upon this theme.

21.1 (Section 57)

A state should be governed in a normal way.
An army should be operated in an unusual way.
The world should be administered by doing nothing.
How do I know that it should be so?
Through the following:
The more prohibitive enactments there are in the world,
    The poorer the people will become;
The more sharp weapons men have,
    The more troubled the state will be;
The more crafts and techniques men possess,
    The more vicious things will appear;
The more laws and orders are made prominent,
    The more robbers and thieves will spring up.
Therefore the sage says:
'I take no action and the people of themselves become transformed.
I love tranquility and the people of themselves become righteous.
I disturb nobody and the people of themselves become prosperous.
I have no desires and the people of themselves become simple.'

Commentary

In this section Laozi proposes three major strategies for three different tasks. The first is the 'normal way' (*zheng*), employed to govern a state; the second is the 'unusual way' (*qi*), applied to operate an army; and the third is the principle of 'take-no-action' (*wu shi*), to administer the world. The first and the third seem to somewhat overlap. They are both intended to stabilize the society and the world. Yet, the second strategy is abnormal in itself, for it is set out in striking contrast to other doctrines including simplicity, non-competition, retreat, and take-no-action, which in effect comprise the main content of Laozi's system of political philosophy.

'All warfare is,' as Sunzi says when talking about strategic assessments in *The Art of War*, 'based on deception. Therefore, when able to attack, we must pretend to be unable; when employing our forces, we must seem inactive; when we are near, we must make the enemy believe we are far away; when far away, we must make him believe we are near. Offer a bait to allure the enemy, when he covets small advantages; strike the enemy when he is in disorder . . . Launch attack where the enemy is unprepared; take action when it is unexpected. These are the keys to victory for a strategist.' These strategies and tactics chime in with Laozi's argument that 'an army should be operated in an unusual or extraordinary way' (*yi qi yong bing*) (1993: 6 [Ch. 1]).

Being a pair of opposite and yet complementary categories, the 'normal way' and the 'unusual way' are not only used by Laozi himself, but by other ancient thinkers, including Sunzi who announces as follows: 'It is due to the operation of the unusual tactics and the normal ones that the whole army can sustain the enemy's all-out attack without suffering defeat.' 'Generally, in battle,' continues Sunzi, 'use the normal force to engage, and use the extraordinary force to win. Now, to a commander adept at the use of extraordinary force, his resources are as infinite as Heaven and Earth, as inexhaustible as the flow of the running rivers . . . In battle, there are not more than two kinds of postures – the operation of the extraordinary way and that of the normal way, but their combinations give rise to an endless line of maneuvers. For these two ways (or forces) are mutually productive. With a circular motion, they never come to an end. Who can exhaust the possibilities of their combinations?' (1993: 18 [Ch. 5]). The use of the interactive combinations between the unusual way and the normal way has been ever since accepted as a law of warfare and put into practice from time to time oblivious to the modernization of weapons of all conceivable kinds.

Human history has witnessed a series of warfare launched out for varied reasons. One of the principal reasons is related to group or nations interests. There often arises a situation as follows: Some of the powerful and greedy people will take advantage of their positions for more gain when swept away by their desires; some of the powerless and the poor people will take risk of theft or robbery when they want more. In order to prevent these mischievous doings some more laws are introduced and exercised in many possible ways.

Nevertheless, the laws are made to break simply because some people tend to violate them in pursuit of their own interest and profit. In the eyes of Laozi, so to speak, nothing can stop the self-seeking people when they rush into their insatiable purposes. They would be influenced to the degree that they may lose the virtue of simplicity and cheat each other.

In order to reduce the occurrence of vicious actions stimulated by greedy desires and prevent people from taking the risk of robbery and theft, Laozi recommends the following four principles applied by the Daoist sage: 'I take no action and the people of themselves become transformed. I love tranquility and the people of themselves become righteous. I disturb nobody and the people of themselves become prosperous. I have no desires and the people of themselves become simple.' Noticeably, by 'transformed' is meant that the people would follow the example of the Daoist sage and conscientiously transform themselves into the good or the innocent via self-cultivation. By 'become simple' is meant that the people will reduce their desires and thus embrace the virtue of simplicity. When taking into due consideration of the harsh reality, we may find the whole idea of Laozi rather idealistic, if not wishful thinking.

21.2 (Section 68)

In the past—
An adept commander did not display his martial prowess.
An adept warrior did not become angry.
An adept conqueror did not tussle with his enemy.
An adept manager of men placed himself below them.
This is called the virtue of non-competition.
This is called the use of others' force.
This is called the supreme principle of matching Heaven.

Commentary

Even in his consideration of military strategies and tactics as presented in this section, Laozi still holds on to his notion that the tender and the soft are bound to overcome the hard and the strong. It is noteworthy that the characters of the adept commander, warrior, and conqueror, and the use of others' forces, all contain dialectical messages relating to the art of war.

Just as Sunzi points out in his remarks on attack by stratagem:

To subdue the enemy without fighting is of supreme excellence. Thus, the best policy in war is to attack the enemy's strategy. The second-best way is to disrupt his alliances through diplomatic means. The next-best method is to attack the enemy in the field. The worst policy is to attack walled cities, since this is the last resort when there is no other alternative . . . Therefore, the adept commander subdues the enemy without confrontation. He captures the enemy's cities without assaulting them and overthrows the enemy's rule without protracted operations . . . However, an adept warrior wins victories without showing his brilliant military prowess (1993: 13–15 [Chs 3–4]).

If we make a close comparison between these ideas about warfare proposed by Sunzi and Laozi, we find them strategically identical in a broad sense in certain cases. It is no wonder that some readers, such as Mao Zedong, take the book of Laozi as one on warfare and applied it to his military exercises during the Anti-Japanese Invasion War and the Civil War alike.

21.3 (Section 69)

In the past, a military strategist said:
'I dare not take the offensive, but I take the defensive.
I dare not advance an inch, but I retreat a foot.'
This means (to make the invading force):
    Advancing onward without battle formation,
    Raising his arm without morale enhancement,
    Holding his weapons without normal function,
    And tackling the enemy without meeting him.
There is no greater disaster than underestimating the enemy.
Such underestimation is tantamount to self-abandonment.
Therefore, when two well-matched armies clash in battle,
    It is the side which retreats first that will win.

Commentary

This section continues to expound upon the crafts of warfare. Under the circumstances, Laozi proposes a number of policies which can be developed and summarized into three major military strategies as follows: (1) wait at one's ease for an exhausted enemy; (2) defend in order to attack; and (3) retreat in order to advance. All these three strategies are intended to 'gain mastery by striking only after the enemy has struck.'

It is noteworthy that a passive stance toward warfare can change into such military strategies as 'wait at one's ease for an exhausted enemy' (*yi yi dai lao*) and 'defend in order to attack' (*yi shou wei gong*). Moreover, the strategy of retreat may lead to positive consequences. This is because whenever confronted in a battle, the invading army tends to be full of strength, and its morale is high at the very beginning so that it seems to be irresistible. Yet, these advantageous elements will gradually fade away if they fail to be put into action as a result of the enemy's avoidance of battle. When the time is ripe, 'retreat in order to advance' (*yi tui wei jin*). However, it must be pointed out that Laozi seems to absolutize the potential power of 'the side which retreats.' It is well known that a military victory or conquest depends on a variety of factors and conditions, and not just on a single policy of retreat or whatsoever. Hence, the absolutization of retreat as a strategy ends up playing down its dialectical content.

It is commendable to scrutinize this section with particular reference to Sunzi's analyses of maneuvering and varied regions covered in *The Art of War*. The two relevant passages are cited in full here:

A whole army may be robbed of its spirit, and its commander deprived of his presence of mind. Now, at the beginning of a campaign, the spirit of soldiers is keen; after a certain period of time, it declines; and in the later stage, it may dwindle to nought. An adept commander, therefore, avoids the enemy when his spirit is keen, and attacks him when it is lost. This is the art of attaching importance to moods. In good order, he awaits a disorderly enemy; in serenity, a clamorous one. This is the art of retaining self-possession. Close to the field of battle, he awaits an enemy coming from afar; at rest, he awaits an exhausted enemy; with well-fed troops, he awaits hungry ones. This is the art of husbanding one's strength. He refrains from intercepting an enemy whose banners are in perfect order, and desists from attacking an enemy whose formations are in impressive array. This is the art of assessing circumstances (1993: 49).

In ancient times, an adept commander knew how to make it impossible for the enemy to unite his van and his rear, for his large and small divisions to cooperate, for his officers and men to support each other, and for the higher and lower levels of the enemy to establish contact with each other. When the enemy's forces were dispersed, the adept commander managed to prevent them from assembling; even when assembled, he managed to throw them into disorder. In this case, the commander led his army to move forward when it was advantageous to do so, and he halted his men when it was disadvantageous to move forward (1993: 79).

Chapter 22

On Peace

Laozi values peace and stability more than anything else in the social domain. This is reflected in his staunch anti-war attitude. Thus he regards weapons as instruments of evil that may be used only when there is no other alternative. He emphasizes that the use of military force is dangerous, for 'as soon as great wars are over, years of famine are sure to afflict the land.' Accordingly he denounces all excessive military operations and discourages any delight in military victory. In addition, he even goes so far as to advise the winning side to cherish humanism by mourning the multitudes killed in the fighting. Laozi's argument on pre-war and post-war peace is presented in Sections 30 and 31 (DDJ).

22.1 (Section 30)

He who assists the ruler with the *Dao*
   Never seeks to dominate the world with military force.
The use of force is intrinsically dangerous:
Wherever armies are stationed,
   Briers and thorns grow wild.
As soon as great wars are over,
   Years of famine are sure to afflict the land.
Therefore an adept commander (of a defensive force) will
   Stop when he has achieved his aim.
He does not use force to dominate the world.
He achieves his aim but does not become arrogant.
He achieves his aim but does not boast about it.
He achieves his aim only because he has no other choice.
This is called achieving the aim without using force to dominate.
The strong and powerful rob and harm the old and weak.
This is called contrary to the *Dao*.
Whatever is contrary to the *Dao* will soon perish.

Commentary

Nothing has been more catastrophic than war in the course of human history. War destroys peace, order, and stability on the one hand, and can cause famine, devastation, and myriads of other miseries on the other. In short, war takes an enormous toll on mankind.

From his own observation and experience of the continual chaos and wars that marked the Spring and Autumn Period, Laozi came to know that the rivalry among the feudal lords striving for ever-more power and territory through the use of military forces led to the disasters of war. However, he could do nothing to stop it, apart from warning people of the dangerous and disastrous aspects of war. Meanwhile, he denounces any excessive military operations by advising the winning side not to go too far (e.g. by colonizing the defeated state and enslaving its people) in their triumph. Otherwise they will betray the *Dao* and, as a consequence, soon perish. World history, for instance, has not merely witnessed the failures of Alexander the Great and Kublai Khan, but also the falls of the Roman Empire and the Third Reich, that all attempted to use force to dominate the world.

22.2 (Section 31)

Weapons are nothing but instruments of evil.
They are used only when there is no other choice.
Therefore, he who wins a battle is not praiseworthy.
If he thinks himself praiseworthy,
    He delights in the victory.
He who delights in the victory,
    Delights in the slaughter of men.
He who delights in the slaughter of men
    Will not succeed under Heaven.
For the multitude killed in the war,
    Let us mourn them with sorrow and grief.
For the victory won by force,
    Let us observe the occasion with funeral ceremonies.

Commentary

This section continues with the discussion of the same theme expounded in the previous one. The denunciation of war and the condemnation of delight in slaughter turn into an appeal for peace in his chaotic and war-torn age. The urging of the winning side or the occupying force not to do further harm to the country and people involved is still of great relevance and significance nowadays. It has been historically proved that it is immensely difficult for the winning side or the occupying force, no matter how powerful it may be, to conquer another nation, even though the latter may be relatively small and weak. Incidentally, Laozi's proposal that the multitude killed in the war should be properly mourned springs from his humanistic ideal. It is coincidentally compatible with the relevant laws and rules of international warfare formulated in modern times.

One of the key arguments Laozi poses here in this section is that 'weapons are nothing but instruments of evil. They are used only when there is no other choice.' Why is it so? It is because 'instruments of evil' (*bu xiang zhi qi*) are those of ill omen and 'companions of death' (*si zhi tu*) in Laozi's terminology. They are so dangerous and detestable that they should be carefully stored instead of being recklessly used. Otherwise they will give rise to great disasters and sufferings. As is known in most cases, wherever any state is fully armed with sharp weapons, it tends to become aggressive and even war-like. For it, blindly or not, believes in its own military strength to silence its people, conquer other states and rake in more gains. Thus thinking critically of sharp weapons as the possible cause of warfare, Laozi asserts that any display of 'sharp weapons' is to be prohibited because it will trigger more problems, as if it serves to open the Pandora's Box.

Chapter 23

On Returning to Antiquity

Laozi assumes that primeval society was characterized by peace, harmony, and stability because the ancients acted in accordance with the *Dao* and embraced simplicity and integrity. Appalled at the social problems and chaotic political situation of his own era, he hankers for the 'good old days' of antiquity, where, he implies, solutions to contemporary problems can be found. The relevant sections are 17, 18, 19, and 65 (DDJ).

23.1 (Section 17)

The best kind of rulers are those whose existence
   Is merely known by the people below them.
The next-best are those who are loved and praised.
The next-best are those who are feared.
The next-best are those who are despised.
If trust in others is not sufficient,
   It will be unrequited.
(The best rulers) are cautious,
   And seldom issue orders.
When tasks are accomplished and affairs completed,
   The common people will say,
   'We simply follow the way of spontaneity.'

Commentary

Laozi expresses in this section his political ideal, which is considered as being drawn and developed from his bitter experience of the harsh reality of his time. On the basis of his concept of the *Dao* of take-no-action as the supreme principle for governance, he distinguishes between four types of rulers. He definitely recommends 'the best kind of rulers' as contrasted to the other three kinds merely because the former conduct state affairs according to the principle of take-no-action or the way of spontaneity.

Throughout his book, Laozi time and again denounces the power-oriented and despotic type of leadership or government, for it will disturb, control, and alienate the people by confusing their minds and spoiling their simplicity. He thus values social stability and order, which he thinks can be possible only when the rulers remain honest and trustworthy, use government as an instrument to serve the people and never use their power to force their will on their subjects. Therefore, Laozi deliberately refers back to the 'good old days' of antiquity as a standard to measure the functions of government of his time. Meanwhile, he strongly objects to rulers who manipulate the people by resorting to all kinds of orders, which are useless in his opinion. Nevertheless, the political ideal that he advocates has obvious Utopian features.

23.2 (Section 18)

When the great *Dao* is rejected,
    The doctrines of humanity and righteousness will arise.
When knowledge and craftiness appear,
    Great hypocrisy will also emerge.
When the six family relations are not in harmony,
    Filial piety and parental affection will be advocated.
When a country falls into chaos,
    Loyal ministers will be praised.

Commentary

Throughout the DDJ text it can be seen that 'the great *Dao*' (*da dao*) is recommended as the one and only solution to all the social problems in antiquity. Yet, reality goes against Laozi's will and develops along its own course. For instance, 'humanity and righteousness' (*ren yi*) are advocated as social values instead of the *Dao* as a remedy for the disorders of the age.

With regard to the harsh condition of his time and in spite of the influence of 'humanity and righteousness' and other values, Laozi deals a sharp attack at them all. His critique is conducted in a roundabout way, coinciding with his notion that 'positive words seem to be negative' (*zheng yan ruo fan*). In the eyes of Laozi, 'humanity and righteousness (*ren yi*), knowledge and craftiness (*zhi hui*), filial piety and parental affection (*xiao ci*), and loyal ministers (*zhong chen*) are all abnormal symptoms of an unhealthy society. So-called moral codes are never properly lived up to in a rational society' (Ren, 1993: 33). This reveals Laozi's dialectical thought about the relations and interactions between the great *Dao*, humanity, righteousness, knowledge, craftiness, hypocrisy, family relations in dispute, filial piety, parental affection, political disorder, and loyal ministers. Historically and realistically speaking, it is fairly true that there must be something out of order whenever those values or morals are in urgent need. They are somewhat like medicine; valuable and desirable as it might be, people take it only when they fall ill. Such being the case, the demand for such a 'good' thing merely indicates the existence of a bad situation.

In this context, 'the great *Dao*' seems to stand for what encompasses the supreme forms of humanity and righteousness, among other values. If the *Dao* of this type is easily available and practiced in a society, there will be simply no need to propagate humanity and righteousness because people are all hoping to live in the harmonious and peaceful atmosphere of the *Dao*.

It must be pointed out that humanity and righteousness (*ren yi*) are typical of Confucianist terminology. That is why some Laozi scholars both in China and overseas opine that Laozi as a thinker appeared after Confucius. They reach such a judgment mainly by means of the Hegelian Triad – thesis, antithesis, and synthesis. That is to say, they deem that 'humanity and righteousness' comprise the thesis, and the critique of it then serves as the antithesis. So logically speaking, Confucius precedes Laozi. Yet, I think that this is a hasty conclusion, for it features a 'leap in dark.' Whenever we approach the history of Chinese thought we ought to keep in mind that Confucius is a Latinized name for Kong Fuzi, a honorific title for Kongzi (a literal translation of which could be Master Kong); likewise, Confucianism is a Latinized term for *Rujia* as the Confucian school of thought. It is widely acknowledged that it was Confucius who developed the thoughts and doctrines of Confucianism. But this does not necessarily mean that it was Confucius who originated all the ideas of Confucianism. In fact, Confucianism as a school of thought existed before Confucius himself, and so did some of the doctrines or theses comprising the early Confucianism, which include 'humanity and righteousness' for example. Confucius claimed that he was a 'transmitter' rather than an originator. This corresponds to historical fact. Nowadays modern studies of Confucianism in China have a general tendency to make a distinction between primitive Confucianism (*Yuanshi Rujia*), Confucianism (*Rujia*), Neo-Confucianism (*Xin Rujia or Song-Ming lixue*), and Modern Confucianism (*Xiandai Ruxue*). We mention all this to justify the conclusion that Laozi preceded Confucius, and not the other way round.

Moreover, the Guodian text as the oldest of all DDJ versions shows a corresponding link between the early Daoism and the early Confucianism. It is expressed in a number of sections. What the subsequent section reveals is a typical example.

When the great *Dao* is rejected,
    How can humanity and righteousness come into being?
When the six family relations are not in harmony,
    How can filial piety and parental affection come into being?
When a country falls into chaos,
    How can upright ministers come into being?

Quite noticeably, all these so-called Confucian values are not negated or blamed as they are in most of the popular DDJ versions ever since Wang Bi's edition. Instead, they are positively treated and expected in view of the premises concerned. The cause-and-effect logic here is identical to that in almost all the Confucian canons. It is therefore argued that the early Daoism and the early Confucianism were set side by side as opponent schools of thought deliberately by those who were against the pretentious aspects of some Confucian ideas. Wang Bi is considered to take the lead in this regard (Guo, 2001: 126–129, 514).

23.3 (Section 19)

Only when sageness is eliminated and craftiness discarded,
    Will people benefit a hundredfold.
Only when humanity is eradicated and righteousness abandoned,
    Will people return to filial piety and parental affection.
Only when skill is thrown away and profit ignored,
    Will there be no more robbers or thieves.
Yet, these three are inadequate as a doctrine.
We therefore urge the following:
    Manifest plainness and embrace simplicity;
    Reduce selfishness and have few desires;
    And get rid of learning and have no worries.

Commentary

As noted in the Section 18 (DDJ), Laozi makes a critical diagnosis of the problematic and somewhat moribund society in his age. He concludes that all the problems arise fundamentally from the rejection of 'the great *Dao*.' He then continues in Section 19 (DDJ) to describe more specifically the pros and cons of such social phenomena as sageness, craftiness, humanity, righteousness, skill, and profit. His negation of them is ostensibly reflected in his arguments and set out in striking contrast to his three proposals as follows: 'manifest plainness and embrace simplicity,' 'reduce selfishness and have few desires,' and 'get rid of learning and have no worries.' It is noticeable that these three proposed solutions to the social problems are proffered in opposition to what Laozi terms 'these three,' pointing to the three pairs of categories: 'sageness and craftiness,' 'humanity and righteousness,' and 'skill and profit.' Laozi actually regards 'these three' as superficial excrescences of civilization advocated at a time when the principle of the *Dao* had been rejected (see 23.2).

In the final analysis, Laozi's proposals are all intended to make it possible for a twofold return: the return to simplicity as the original human nature or the highest stage of self-cultivation, and the return to antiquity as an idealized social living environment.

Incidentally, we must keep in mind the fact that Laozi denies and condemns 'sageness and craftiness' because they produce self-importance and misused intelligence which tend to endanger human relations, 'humanity and righteousness' because they produce vanity, pretentiousness, and hypocrisy, which tend to disguise base intentions, and 'skill and profit' in view of prevailing trickiness and overflowing desires, which tend to stir up more troubles.

23.4 (Section 65)

In ancient times he who practiced the *Dao* well
   Did not use it to enlighten the people.
Instead he used it to make them simple.
Now the people are difficult to govern
   Because they have too much craftiness.
Thus, governing a country by craftiness is a disaster for it.
And not governing it by craftiness is a blessing for it.
He who knows these two also knows the principle.
It is called the profound *De* to always know the principle.
The profound *De* is deep and far-reaching;
It returns to the origin with all things,
   And then leads to the great naturalness.

Commentary

It is difficult to rule those who have too many desires, and equally difficult to rule those who have too much craftiness. It is Laozi's conviction that people become so mainly because they are under the negative influence of the ruling class. Hence, he believes that the leaders should first of all set themselves up as good models of simplicity and genuineness in their styles of both governing and living. Then it will be possible for the people to become simple and genuine, or, in short, easy to rule. Subsequently, human relations can be improved, and social stability maintained.

As a matter of fact, Laozi was born in a chaotic age which featured political conflicts and military clashes between the states across ancient China. Moreover, in fighting and power games within the courts of the states were an ever-present complication in the process of government. The result was an eager pursuit of stratagems, tricks, and conspiracies. Under such circumstances, he found the chief cause of confusion and disorder lay in nothing but craftiness, trickiness, competitiveness, and hypocrisy. He therefore called on people to get rid of all forms of struggle and dispute related to possessive values, and advised them to return to the mentality of genuineness and simplicity, which he held to be the key to the solutions to all the crises of his time. In order to hammer this point home to the reader, his remarks are noticeably sharp and cynical (Chen, 1992: 315).

As regards the tactics for governance proposed by Laozi, they tend to be understood as a kind of obscurantism. They are thus approached by the rulers of almost all the dynasties in China with particular reference to the similar arguments presented in Section 3 (DDJ), as follows: 'Therefore the sage governs the people by purifying their minds, filling their bellies, weakening their ambitions, and strengthening their bones' (see 20.1).

Chapter 24

On the Ideal Society

Throughout his book, Laozi proposes the principle of the *Dao*, advocates simplicity of mind, appreciates the environment of tranquility, denounces the catastrophe of war, and admires the community in antiquity. All these elements naturally lead to his conception of the ideal society characterized by 'a small state with few people.' It is ostensibly out of the range of feasibility or possibility. It is therefore taken as a spiritual refuge for those who tend to frown upon over-civilization and shun the problematic world.

24.1 (Section 80)

Let there be a small state with few people.
It has various kinds of instruments,
   But let none of them be used.
Let the people not risk their lives, and not migrate far away.
Although they have boats and carriages,
   Let there be no occasion to ride in them.
Although they have armor and weapons,
   Let there be no occasion to display them.
Let the people return to knotting cords and using them.
Let them relish their food,
   Beautify their clothing,
   Feel comfortable in their homes
   And delight in their customs.
Although the neighboring states are within sight of one another,
   And the crowing of cocks and the barking of dogs
   On both sides can be heard,
   Their peoples may die of old age without even meeting each other.

Commentary

Exemplified in this section is Laozi's ideal society that features 'a small state with few people.' As has been observed, the small state as such is basically structured on the model of a community in antiquity, and the people living there are simple, honest, and peace-loving by nature. They remain contented with what they have, and thereby live enjoyable lives. There are no disputes or conflicts among the neighboring states because they all take care of their own affairs without bothering each other. This social ideal was later on extended by Tao Yuanming, an influential poet (c. 372 or 376–427), into a Chinese Utopia known as Peach Blossom Village (*Tao Hua Yuan*), which is in fact the title of a literary essay of his.

Noticeably, Laozi's ideal society is a natural outcome of his admiration for antiquity, his advocacy of simplicity, his appreciation of tranquility, his anti-war attitude, his pursuit of stability, and, above all, his principle of the *Dao*. It goes without saying that Laozi fictionalizes and idealizes such a society, which is in sharp contrast to the harsh and chaotic reality of his time. He lauds such an ideal society while implicitly criticizing the traits of acquisitiveness, vanity, and competitiveness found in human nature. Obviously his ideal society is far beyond actualization. It thus serves as a spiritual refuge for those who are disgusted with the over-civilized world.

It is generally acknowledged that Laozi calls for a return to the primitive community, as exemplified in his idealized society. However, it is a kind of return at a higher level with regard to the following characteristics:

First of all, Laozi's idealized society is similar to the primitive community in the aspects of equality, co-production, shared consumption, non-possessiveness, and non-control. Yet, the former is different from the latter to the extent that it is governed by 'taking no action' and following the way of naturalness. As a result, people there do not need to run the risk of leaving home in order to make a living elsewhere.

Secondly, in the idealized society of Laozi, there are various kinds of instruments – boats, carriages, armor, weapons, and so forth – which were scarcely available to the primitive community. They are hardly used because there is no occasion for using them. This denotes that the members of this ideal society stick to simplicity in their activities, and free from clashes or warfare between the communities.

Thirdly, primitive society featured low productivity and low living standards, such that there was scarcely any access to the pleasures of life. However, the society idealized by Laozi is characterized with a considerable quality of life. For it makes it possible for people to 'relish their food, beautify their clothing, feel comfortable in their homes, and delight in their customs.'

Finally, the proposed solution to 'let the people return to knotting cords and using them' should not be simplistically conceived of as an idea to restore the outdated and retreat to the past. More exactly, it is an attempt to use the innocence and simplicity of antiquity to supersede the craftiness, trickery, and hypocrisy of the people in Laozi's age. In short, the ideal society bears such characteristics as equality, self-sufficiency, security, simplicity, peaceful coexistence, tranquility, harmony, and an idyllic life above all, which has been dreamed of or cherished in either the human imagination or wishful thinking.

Chapter 25

The Attitude to the Dao and the De

Daoism as a philosophy is often reckoned to be the wellspring of the psychology of the Chinese people in general. This is due to the fact that Daoism is largely directed toward personal cultivation from within, which is then chiefly oriented to the attainment of the Dao and the De as the highest sphere of human life. Laozi proclaims that 'the Dao begets all beings and the De fosters them . . . Therefore all beings venerate the Dao and honor the De.' When cultivated and exercised in the person, family, community, country, and the world at large, both the Dao and the De will become genuine, overflowing, everlasting, powerful, and universal. Thereby, the entire world will stay in peace and order, and mankind will enjoy harmonious relations.

There are generally three different kinds of attitudes toward the Dao and the De categorized by Laozi. The first is positive and held by the highest type of *literati* (*shi*); the second is doubtful and held by the average type of *literati*; and the last is negative and held by the lowest type of *literati*. Personal cultivation in Daoism depends, first and foremost, on an appropriate attitude to the Dao and the De. Close reading of Sections 41 and 70 (DDJ) may give one some basic ideas in this case.

25.1 (Section 41)

When the highest type of *literati* hear of the Dao,
    They diligently practice it.
When the average type of *literati* hear of the Dao,
    They half-believe it.
When the lowest type of *literati* hear of the Dao,
    They laugh heartily at it.
If they did not laugh at it,
    It would not be the Dao.

Therefore there is the established saying:
    The Dao that is bright seems to be dark;

The *Dao* that advances seems to retreat;
The *Dao* that is level seems to be uneven.
Thus the great *De* appears empty like a valley;
The far-reaching *De* appears insufficient;
The vigorous *De* appears inert;
The simplistic *De* appears clumsy;
The whitest appears soiled;
The greatest square has no corners;
The greatest vessel is unfinished;
The greatest music sounds faint;
The greatest form has no shape;
The *Dao* is hidden and nameless.
Yet it is the *Dao* that initiates all things
And brings them to completion.

Commentary

Laozi classifies *literati* (*shi*) as a social stratum into three broad types: the highest, the average, and the lowest. Their respective attitudes toward the *Dao* reflect three general attitudes. It is obvious that Laozi holds a positive and commendable view of the first of the three attitudes to the *Dao* and the *De*. In order to clear away the doubts and ignorance the average *literati* and the lowest *literati* have as regards the *Dao*, Laozi cites some old sayings (that could be created by himself) to testify to the authentic and extraordinary functions of the *Dao* and the *De*. As can be observed nowadays in this world where materialism and nihilism are so prevalent and rampant, plenty of people are inclined to sneer or mock at the *Dao* of human conduct characterized by such *De* as simplicity, honesty, morality, selflessness, and so forth. Many people seem to get lost or confused in respect of their value systems. With regard to this, the implied message in this section is noticeably of considerable relevance and significance since it encourages the development of the highest type of *literati* with an affirmative attitude to the *Dao* and the *De*.

By the way, the line that 'the greatest vessel is unfinished' (*da qi mian cheng*) is modified according to one of the two Mawangdui DDJ versions, for it fits better in the context. The greatest vessel as an instrument would be too large to have any fixed form or function. It is thus beyond human capacity to either use it or complete it. In most of the popular DDJ versions, the line reads: *da qi wan cheng* and it is thus translated as 'the greatest vessel is always completed last.'

Interestingly, the greatest music is in fact the most fascinating and beautiful music that only exists in one's imagination. In practice what is composed cannot fully express what is imagined; and what is performed can hardly be any better than what is composed. This is merely because the original beauty and charm get more or less lost during the transition from creative imagination to instrumental performance. For this reason, Tao Yuanming preferred to play the Chinese lute without cords. Coincidentally, John Keats remarks in one of his poems titled *Ode on a Grecian Urn* as follows:

Heard melodies are sweet
But those unheard are sweeter
Therefore, ye soft pipes, play on
Not to the sensual ear, but more endear'd
Pipe to the spirit ditties of no tone . . .

25.2 (Section 70)

All the world says that my *Dao* is great,
  But it does not resemble anything concrete.
Just because it is great,
  It does not resemble anything concrete.
It would have been small for long if it did.

My words are very easy to understand and practice.
But no one in the world can understand and practice them.
My words have their own source.
My deeds have their own master.
It is merely because people do not know this
  That they fail to understand me.
Those who can understand me are very few,
  And those who can follow me are hard to meet.
Therefore the sage wears coarse garb,
  But conceals a precious jade in his bosom.

Commentary

In this section Laozi seems to be somewhat anguished because his ideas are not appreciated and his deeds not followed by the majority. He ascribes this frustrating situation to human ignorance of the *Dao* and its manifestations. However, the reluctance to act upon his words and deeds lies, in my opinion, in the tendency of many people to become blinded with acquisitiveness and pleasure-snobbery. As a result they fix their eyes either on the dazzling appearances or the practical dimensions of things, and naturally neglect the spiritual aspect, as exemplified by the inner and virtuous self.

Generally speaking, personal cultivation in Daoism depends on the willingness to modify one's behavior and purify one's mind on the model embodied via the Daoist sage. This requires a sincere consideration of the words and deeds of the sage. Naturally the most important thing is to foster and establish a positive attitude toward the *Dao* and the *De* just like that held by the highest type of *literati* discussed above.

As can be noted in the last two lines – 'the sage wears coarse garb, but conceals a precious jade in his bosom' – there contains a metaphor rich in meaning. It implies first of all the personality of the Daoist sage that features plainness and simplicity, without any intention to show off himself. Secondly, the 'coarse garb' signifies the outside appearance which serves to cover up the 'precious jade.' The 'jade' in this context stands for the *Dao* and the *De* as well.

Incidentally, the original statement in this section runs as '*zhi wo zhe xi, ze wo zhe gui*.' The first part (*zhi wo zhe xi*) means 'those who can understand [or know] me are very few.' Regarding Laozi's doctrine of the *Dao*, it is difficult for people to understand it, and it is even more difficult for people to act upon it. This being the case, the second part (*ze wo zhe gui*) is put into 'those who can follow me are hard to meet.' It can be paraphrased as 'those who can follow me are even fewer.' The expression 'very few' means that there are still a couple of persons who understand Laozi's doctrine of the *Dao*. In contrast, the expression 'hard to meet' means that Laozi hardly finds anyone to take up his doctrine of the *Dao*. Needless to say, the English rendering is open to further improvement, but the basic idea is as it seems to be like this at the present stage. The word 'follow' is derived from the Chinese word '*ze*' that also means 'adhere to' or 'act upon.' The expression 'hard to meet' is derived from the Chinese character '*gui*' that also mean 'be rare, scarce, dear or precious.'

Chapter 26

The Experience of the Dao and the De

As a result of adopting a positive attitude to the *Dao* and the *De*, one would undergo a highly enlightened experience and even mental change which is uniquely distinct from and well transcends any practical or empirical types. This kind of experience and mentality features above all simplicity, tranquility, genuineness, modesty, adaptability, open-mindedness, and persistency, which in turn represent the fundamental aspects of the ideal personality Laozi advocates. A scrutiny of Sections 15 and 20 (DDJ) will offer some insights into this topic.

26.1 (Section 15)

He who was adept at practicing the *Dao* in antiquity
   Was subtly profound and penetrating, too deep to be understood.
As he was beyond people's cognitive capacity,
   I can only describe him arbitrarily:
He was cautious, as if walking across a frozen river in winter;
He was vigilant, as if being threatened by an attack on all sides;
He was solemn and reserved, like a visiting guest;
He was supple and pliant, like ice about to melt;
He was broad, like the boundless sea;
He was vigorous, like the untiring blowing wind;
He was genuine and plain, like the uncarved block;
He was open and expansive, like a great valley;
He was merged and indifferent, like muddy water
Who could make the muddy gradually clear via tranquility?
Who could make the still gradually come to life via activity?
(It was nobody else but him.)
He who maintains the *Dao* does not want to be overflowing.
It is just because he does not want to be overflowing
   That he can be renewed when worn out.

Commentary

This section presents Laozi's description of the experience of the men who supposedly followed the *Dao*. The *Dao* is too subtle and profound to be understood by the ordinary man. Accordingly, he who is good at practicing the *Dao* is also 'subtly profound and penetrating, too deep to be understood' by the common people.

As far-fetched a depiction as it is in Laozi's terms, the experience of a highly enlightened type is a process of encountering and handling a variety of conditions. This process is in effect a process of personal cultivation, featuring such manners and frames of mind as cautiousness, vigilance, solemnity, adaptability, plainness, simplicity, genuineness, broad-mindedness, receptivity, tranquility, persistency, vitality, enduringness, boundlessness, modesty, and so on. These are actually the essential dimensions of an ideal personality in Laozi's view. Comparatively speaking, these two rhetorical questions – Who could make the muddy gradually clear via tranquility? Who could make the still gradually come to life via activity? – contain a very crucial and instructive message. They at least expose the difficulty related to the experience and practice of the *Dao* and the *De* during the process of which tranquility and patience are highly demanded but hard to be maintained and exercised with persistency and continuity. 'The muddy' has rich connotations. On one level it means 'muddy water,' but metaphorically it signifies a muddy mind, turbid situation, chaotic order, confused environment, and decadent morality. All this is the opposite of 'the clear' as its antithesis. Likewise, 'the still' is regarded as denoting 'the dead,' 'the static,' 'the inert,' and 'the inactive.' All this is antithetical to the qualities of 'the alive' or 'the dynamic.' As regards these two pairs of opposite categories – the muddy and the clear, the still and the alive – a vehicle of transformation is highly desirable. The vehicle itself seems to be made up of such essential but contradictory elements as 'tranquility' and 'activity,' as recommended by Laozi.

As has often been observed in practice and experience, it is through concentration and tranquility that one is able to get out of the mire of muddiness and confusion on the one hand, and eventually become clear-minded and remain at ease on the other. This is often true of the natural process during which muddy water becomes clear through tranquility or freedom from disturbance. Whenever one calms down and keeps oneself in a state of tranquility, his rationality, judgment, and feeling will all work clearly, rationally, and pleasantly. However, in terms of psychology and development, the involvement in tranquility and peace for too long a time can turn into a state of stillness, during which one may grow slack, inert, or indolent. At this stage activity is required as a stimulus. When activated and motivated, one becomes renewed, energetic, and creative again. This can be seen as an exposition of the reason why stillness (static state) taken to its extreme degree will turn into activity (dynamic state) and vice versa in the existence of all beings. The dialectical form of their transformation is actually extended from the general principle that 'reversion is the movement of the *Dao*' (DDJ, Sect. 40).

It is said that the philosopher Martin Heidegger (1889–1976) was deeply impressed by the two lines quoted above. He had them written on a wall scroll and hung it in his study for contemplation. We guess that the German philosopher may have had his own reason to do so, because he himself was at the time preoccupied with seeking the possibility of 'clarity.'

Incidentally, many Laozi scholars tend to annotate these two lines from their respective perspectives and experiences. Take Wang Bi and Heshang Gong, for example. The former views them as explaining natural phenomena which demonstrate the working of the *Dao* of spontaneity or naturalness, whereas the latter assumes that they reflect the human state and process of becoming in both a mental and physical sense. Modern Laozi scholars also supply different annotations. With regard to the Chinese term *zhuo*, Wu Chen, Chen Guying, and others hold that it implies a state of stirring or turbulence (Chen, 1992: 120); Sha Shaohai and others reckon that it indicates a chaotically turbid and rigid environment in a social or psychical dimension (Sha, 1992: 26–27). Some scholars maintain that it refers to 'muddy water.' That is why we encounter such English renderings as follows: 'Which of you can assume such murkiness, to become in the end still and clear? Which of you can make yourself inert, to become in the end full of life and stir?' (Waley, 1994: 31–33). 'Who can make the muddy water clear? As it quiets down it will become clear. Who can make stillness last? It will gradually lose its peace as change arises' (Ren, 1993: 29). 'Who can make muddy water gradually clear through tranquility? Who can make the still gradually come to life through activity?' (Chan, 1973: 147). I personally agree with Chan and Ren, as I think Laozi uses the word *zhuo* as a metaphor which corresponds to the characteristics of his empirical observation and intuitive thinking as a whole. Comparatively speaking, Wing-tsit Chan's version is more concise and closer to Laozi's style. Here I have changed 'muddy water' into 'the muddy' owing to my conviction that it is more suggestive in the physical, social, mental, and moral senses, in addition to its going parallel to 'the still' as a collective noun employed therein.

26.2 (Section 20)

How much difference is there between ready approval
    And outright denunciation?
How much difference is there between good and evil?
What people fear cannot but be feared.
The multitude are merry, as if feasting on a day of sacrifice,
    Or as if ascending a tower to enjoy the scenery in springtime.
I alone remain tranquil and reluctant to distinguish.
I feel broad and far-reaching, as if at a loss;

I am indifferent and without concern,
    Like an infant that cannot smile;
I am wearied indeed,
    As if I have no home to return to.
The multitude are so brilliant and self-exhibiting,
    I alone seem to be lost in darkness and ignorance.
The multitude are so observant and discriminating,
    I alone intend to make no distinctions.
The multitude possess more than enough,
    I alone seem to lack everything.
The multitude have their reasons for taking action,
    I alone seem to be clumsy and incapable of nothing.
The multitude like to be endorsed and supported,
    I alone value the realization and attainment of the *Dao*.

Commentary

This section represents Laozi's attitude to society and life in general. He thinks it rather relative and tentative with regard to the judgment of such values as nobility and humility, good and evil, beautiful and ugly. Therefore, he remains reluctant to distinguish between the so-called distinctions which are casually made by the multitude.

It is noticeable that Laozi could not display much tolerance for the society of his era. He looked upon the multitude as being mean, base, vulgar, and shameless . . . In the last sentence he shows that the difference between this 'I' and others is that the former has achieved the *Dao* while the latter has not. Laozi himself objects to the dedication to a pleasure-seeking kind of life, which is a symptom of materialism or over-civilization. He exposes his way of life in order to encourage the multitude to devote themselves to spiritual nourishment instead of material possessions or physical enjoyment. He is thus different from others due to the fact that he is persistent in his pursuit of the *Dao* as his ultimate goal in life.

Chapter 27

The Praxis of the Dao *and the* De

The praxis of the *Dao* and the *De* involves relevant strategies articulated in the subsequent sections. The benefits of acting upon the *Dao* as the supreme principle and nourishing the *De* as the highest virtue are extensive and boundless according to Laozi; better still, they are accessible and available to all beings alike under Heaven. Let us focus on Sections 7, 23, and 27, with reference to Sections 35, 52, and 54 (DDJ).

27.1 (Section 7)

Heaven is eternal and Earth everlasting.
They can be so just because they do not exist for themselves.
And for this reason they can long endure.
Therefore the sage places himself in the background,
    But finds himself in the foreground
He puts himself away without self-consideration,
    And yet he always remains well-preserved.
It is because he has no personal interests
    That his personal interests are fulfilled.

Commentary

Some Laozi readers argue that this section reveals a crafty and diplomatic egoism. In other words, Laozi is thought to advocate taking no action for oneself simply because that is the easiest way to gain profit, or attaining selfish ends through selflessness. On the other hand, some other Laozi readers maintain that this section exemplifies a kind of objective law, as does Section 36 (DDJ). Hence, they argue that it is only natural for the Daoist sage to 'find himself in the foreground,' 'remain well-preserved' and have his personal interests come to fruition simply because of his modesty and selflessness.

 As a matter of fact, Laozi's description of Heaven and Earth in view of their alleged selflessness is allegorically directed toward the personality of the Daoist sage. It is largely due to his virtuous modesty and selflessness that the sage can be a beloved ruler and long endure. In reality, however, many rulers fail to restrain their selfish desires owing to external temptations and easy access to treasured objects or rare things. Bit by bit they get deeply involved in corruption and other forms of social ills. When they go too far in order to satisfy their greed at the expense of the interests of the majority, they are likely to be either overthrown or punished in the end. That is why Laozi advises people to follow the example of the sage by means of a genuine practice of the *Dao* and the *De*, both in word and deed.

27.2 (Section 23)

A whirlwind does not last a whole morning;
A rainstorm does not last a whole day.
What causes them to be so? It is Heaven and Earth.
If Heaven and Earth cannot make them last long,
    How much less can man?
Therefore, he who seeks the *Dao* is identified with the *Dao*.
He who seeks the *De* is identified with the *De*.
He who seeks Heaven is identified with Heaven.
He who is identified with the *Dao*—
    The *Dao* is also happy to have him.
He who is identified with the *De*—
    The *De* is also happy to have him.
He who is identified with Heaven—
    Heaven is also happy to have him.

Commentary

This section explains the way to master the *Dao* by virtue of faithful practice and bilateral identification. In plain language, if one pursues the *Dao* with faith, he will attain it and identify himself with it by applying it to his actions. The concept of the oneness between man and the *Dao*, man and the *De* as well as man and Heaven (i.e. Nature) is a thread that runs throughout the historical development of Chinese thought in general, and underlies the spirit of Chinese philosophy in particular.

It is of great significance that Laozi criticizes, albeit in a roundabout way, the severe laws, strict regulations, heavy taxation, and forced labor that afflict the people in a country under despotic rule, for such measures often do more harm than good. Moreover, their very harshness ensures that such measures are short-lived! As has been noted, it is from his philosophy of keeping to tranquility and governing by non-action that Laozi offers his implied criticism, intending to warn the ruling class not to take any arbitrary or drastic actions in view of governance or leadership. Otherwise, they are doomed to failure.

27.3 (Section 27)

He who is adept at traveling leaves no track or trace behind.
He who is adept at speaking makes no blemishes or flaws.
He who is adept at counting uses no tallies or counters.
He who is adept at shutting the door needs no bolts,
    And yet it cannot be opened when shut.
He who is adept at binding things needs no strings,
    And yet they cannot be untied when bound.

Commentary

This section exemplifies the advantage and validity of practicing the *Dao* and the *De*. It seems to Laozi that all human affairs could be well done as naturally as possible provided one follows and acts upon the supreme principle of the *Dao*. The depiction of being adept at traveling and speaking is in fact an extended notion of Laozi's thesis as regards 'taking no (arbitrary) action' and 'teaching without using (fine-sounding) words.'

It is worth pointing out that the advantages of practicing the *Dao* and the *De* are reflected and stated here and there throughout the DDJ. A wise ruler, for instance, will have all the people under Heaven come to him if he holds fast to the Great Image, which is another name for the *Dao* (see 2.2). The people in general will be free from danger throughout their lives if they have found and still keep to the *Dao* as the mother of the universe (see 15.3). Talking about the *De*, it will become pure and genuine when cultivated and exercised in the person, full and overflowing when cultivated and exercised in the family, constant and everlasting when cultivated and exercised in the community, powerful and abundant when cultivated and exercised in the country, universal and all-embracing when cultivated and exercised in the world (see 7.1).

Chapter 28

The Attainment of the Dao *and the* De

It is notable that Laozi talks about the *Dao* from various perspectives throughout his book. One of the most important objectives lies in how to pursue the *Dao* as the highest sphere or realm of the human spirit. As a matter of fact, the pursuit of the *Dao* is implied in certain proposals as hidden in his discussion of the *Dao* and its characteristics. It is worth mentioning that the pursuit of the *Dao* reflects the Daoist ideal of human life. In order to illustrate Laozi's approach to attaining the *Dao*, we presume to break down his approach to the *Dao* and the *De* into six components as follows: self-purification and deep contemplation, plainness and simplicity, vacuity and tranquility, tenderness and non-competition, have-less-selfishness and have-few-desires, and naturalness and take-no-action.

The idea of 'self-purification and deep contemplation' is a modified version of Laozi's notion (*di chu xuan jian*) initially presented in Section 10 (DDJ). One may as well go on to read Sections 47 and 52 (DDJ) so as to achieve a better understanding of how to purify one's mind and contemplate things in a similar form of insightful meditation. The approach as such is, needless to say, oriented toward the mastery of the *Dao* and the nourishment of the *De*.

The subject matter of Section 28 (DDJ) is to stress 'the perception of plainness and the embracing of simplicity' (*jian su bao pu*). It is taken directly from Section 19 (DDJ, see 23.3) and proposed by Laozi himself as an approach to the attainment of the *Dao*. As a matter of fact, simplicity is another name for the *Dao*, which features naturalness, innocence, and purity. It seems minute, simple, and clumsy, yet, it can be so powerful that nothing under Heaven can subdue it. Therefore, if the rulers were able to maintain it, all the people would submit to them spontaneously (see 4.2).

The idea of 'keeping to vacuity and tranquility' (*zhi xu shou jing*) is recommended in Section 16 (DDJ) as two major principles for self-cultivation on the one hand, and for the attainment of the *Dao* and the nourishment of the *De* on the other. The application of these two principles is expected to purify the mind of all conventional prejudices and egoistic desires. At the same time, one can free oneself from all self-indulgence and external disturbances as well as material temptations. By so doing one is able to return to the root as the state of tranquility, to the destiny as the originally good nature, and to the eternal as the everlasting and supreme principle of the *Dao*. As a consequence, he will be identified with the *Dao*, the *De*, and Heaven; that is, he will then achieve the highest form of life in a spiritual sense. This argument is presented in Section 16 (DDJ).

Laozi firmly grounds his doctrine of keeping to tenderness (*shou rou*) on his conviction that 'reversion is the movement of the *Dao*.' Thus he believes that the tender, the soft, and the weak are companions of life, and able to overcome the hard, stiff, and strong. They are described as companions of death in his terminology. Conquest of this kind is only possible in Laozi's opinion when the *De* of non-competition (*bu zheng*) is concretely applied as a code of conduct to practice with sincerity and modesty. It requires therefore such indispensable traits as 'not clinging to one's opinions,' 'not claiming to be always right,' and 'not boasting of one's prowess,' which are all stressed in Section 22 (DDJ).

Presented in Section 19 (DDJ) is the idea of 'reducing one's selfishness and having few desires' (*shao si gua yu*) in order to approach the *Dao* as the model for the world. As has been read in his book, Laozi respectively recommends having less selfishness by forgetting one's body and having few desires by developing a state of infancy. If one's self-cultivation reaches this stage, one is well on the path to the attainment of the *Dao* and the *De* together. The approach to have-less-selfishness and have-few-desires is emphasized in Sections 13 and 49 (DDJ).

Laozi proclaims that the *Dao* 'follows the way of spontaneity or naturalness' (*dao fa zi ran*) (DDJ, Sects 25, 22) and features 'take-no-action' (*wu wei*) (DDJ, Sects 37, 38, and 48). In turn, these characteristic elements could be taken up as an approach to achieving the *Dao*. The application of this approach can be effective only when the pursuit of the *Dao* is firmly established as the ultimate goal of life. A relevant and instructive message is contained in Section 48 (DDJ).

28.1 (Section 10)

Can you keep the spirit and embrace the One
  Without departing from them?
Can you concentrate your vital energy and achieve tenderness
  Like an infant without any desires?
Can you purify your mind and contemplate in depth
  Without any flecks?
Can you love the people and govern the state
  Without taking action?
Can you play the role of the feminine
  In the opening and closing of the gates of Heaven?
Can you understand all and penetrate all
  Without using your reasoning powers?

Commentary

This section centers upon the approach to personal cultivation in the direction of attaining the *Dao* as the highest form of life. The unity of the body and the soul signifies the identification of man with the *Dao*. The realization of this unity will naturally lead to the harmony or harmonious development of one's body (i.e. physical and emotional life) and soul (spiritual and rational life).

It is noteworthy that vital energy (*qi*) is either the source or force of life itself. Ancient Chinese philosophers and doctors believed that life appears when this vital energy gathers, whereas death occurs when it disperses. This notion bears such a historical impact that many Chinese people are still convinced that diseases result from a blocked or problematic flow of this vital energy in the meridians or the channels and collaterals (*jing luo*) of the human body. To concentrate one's vital energy and obtain infant-like tenderness will inevitably lead to a peaceful and calm state of mind (*xin ping qi he*) as a healthy psychical environment, which is in fact the companion of life and ensures freedom from worries and cares.

Self-purification and deep contemplation will help one get rid of all selfish desires and considerations in one sense, and in another sense, help one achieve deep and profound insights into all things. In short, these two strategies for personal cultivation will surely end up in great wisdom and even the mastery of the *Dao*. Mastery of the *Dao* in a social sense produces the Daoist sage, who can 'love the people and govern the state without taking action.'

It is interesting to imagine that it might be possible, by means of self-purification and deep contemplation, to know the 'all-under-Heaven' and see the *Dao* of Heaven without going out of the door or looking through the window (see 15.2). In order to achieve this, Laozi advises people to 'block the vent and close the door' (see 15.3) so as to attain serene contemplation and insightful observation.

28.2 (Section 28)

He who knows the masculine and keeps to the feminine
    Will become the ravine of the world
Being the ravine of the world,
    He will never depart from the constant *De*,
    But return to the state of infancy.
He who knows glory but keeps to disgrace
    Will become the valley of the world.
Being the valley of the world,
    He will be proficient in the constant *De*
    And return to the state of simplicity.
He who knows the white but keeps to the black

Will become the principle of the world.
Being the principle of the world,
    He will possess the constant *De*
    And return to the state of ultimate infinity.
(When the simplicity is broken up,
    It is turned into vessels.
By using these vessels,
    The sage becomes the head of officials.
Hence a perfect government is not carved out of artificiality.)

Commentary

In this section Laozi resorts to a number of symbols to round out the plain and simplistic aspects of the *Dao*. 'The masculine' symbolizes the hard, strong, active, aggressive, and dynamic, while 'the feminine' symbolizes the tender, weak, passive, regressive, and static. In short, these two terms are respectively equivalent in symbolism to a pair of Chinese philosophical categories known as the *Yang* and the *Yin*. Laozi is apt to recommend his notion of the feminine for its reserved character and its potential power. This is compatible with his idea that 'weakness is the function of the *Dao*,' and similarly with his conviction that 'the tender and the weak conquer the hard and the strong.'

Both 'ravine' and 'valley' serve as symbols of modesty and emptiness with the capability to accommodate all things. Meanwhile they tend to suggest that they are by no means competitive or exhibitionist. They are ready to absorb, and not repel, whatever comes to them.

'The state of infancy' indicates innocence and purity of mind and spirit. 'The state of simplicity' implies perfect and natural simplicity, like a block of uncarved wood. In a mental state of simplicity, one is usually immune from any acquisitive desires or competitive instincts. Thus he may enjoy peace and harmony with his surroundings. The last line of this section advises the ruler or government to put into practice the ideal of simplicity as the highest principle. Only by so acting will he be able to hold on to the *Dao* with integrity.

It is noticeable that Laozi uses the word 'return' (*fu gui*) from time to time. The final destination that the Daoist sage is expected to return to is claimed to signify a hierarchy of three interrelated spheres of mentality. These spheres are respectively depicted as 'the state of infancy' (plainness and innocence), 'the state of the uncarved block' (purity and simplicity), and 'the state of ultimate infinity' (the original *Dao*). The last sphere is the highest of all, because he who returns to that state of ultimate infinity is identified, or becomes one with the *Dao*. To attain this objective there must be a medium that is thought to lie in the persistent and deliberate decreasing of desires and selfishness. Sections 19 and 32 (DDJ) cast a particular light on Laozi's advocacy of plainness and simplicity.

28.3 (Section 16)

Try the utmost to get the heart into complete vacuity.
Be sure to keep the mind in steadfast tranquility.
All things are growing and developing
   And I see thereby their cycles
Though all things flourish with a myriad of variations,
   Each one eventually returns to its root.
This returning to its root is called tranquility;
This tranquility is called returning to its destiny;
Returning to its destiny is called the eternal.
To know the eternal is called enlightenment and wisdom.
Not to know the eternal is to take blind action,
   Thus resulting in disaster.
He who knows the eternal can embrace all.
He who embraces all can be impartial.
He who is impartial can be all-encompassing.
He who is all-encompassing can be at one with Heaven
He who is at one with Heaven can be at one with the *Dao*.
He who is at one with the *Dao* can be everlasting
   And free from danger throughout his life.

Commentary

This section centers on the importance of how to foster and keep vacuity and tranquility as a source of spiritual nourishment and personal cultivation. Psychologically speaking, the principle of vacuity is intended to reduce and eradicate self-indulgence and egoistic arrogance in one sense, and to develop a capacity to embrace all things in another. Likewise, the principle of tranquility is meant to help a person diminish and free himself from self-opinionated-ness and prejudice that tend to cause mental confusion and disturbances. Only by means of vacuity and tranquility can one absorb more vital energy and preserve oneself well, in addition to being able to return to 'the root,' 'the destiny,' and 'the eternality' in Laozi's terminology. The notion of tranquility is repeatedly emphasized in the DDJ. In view of its potentiality, Laozi asserts that 'the tranquil overcomes the hasty ... By remaining quiet and tranquil, one can become the ruler of the world' (DDJ, Sect. 45, also see 14.5).

As regards returning to 'the root,' it means to return to the origin of all beings, which refers to the *Dao* and features vacuity and tranquility. Associated with returning to 'the root' is the idea of returning to 'destiny,' from which the Neo-Confucian doctrine of 'returning to the original nature of man' is derived and developed. Some Neo-Confucianists in the Song Dynasty (960–1279) were convinced that the human mind or nature is originally clear, pure, and transparent. It becomes perplexed, confused, and soiled because it is covered with social dust, influences, bias, ambitions, acquired craftiness, and so forth. Thus it is through sincere reflection on the inner self and self-correction of egoistic ills that one can be able to return to one's original good nature.

Laozi's concept of being at one with Heaven and the *Dao* is further discussed in Section 23 (DDJ). We may cite it here for further consideration: 'He who seeks the *Dao* is identified with the *Dao*. He who seeks the *De* is identified with the *De*. He who seeks Heaven is identified with Heaven. He who is identified with the *Dao* – The *Dao* is also happy to have him. He who is identified with the *De* – The *De* is also happy to have him. He who is identified with Heaven – Heaven is also happy to have him.'

In order to understand the section from a wider perspective, it is worth citing the following comments: 'In this section Laozi advocates emptying the mind and maintaining an impartial attitude toward change and development. From his point of view changes are no more than cyclical movement. A change will eventually come back to its point of departure. This is called *gui-gen* (returning to the root). In the final analysis, motion is not different from changelessness, that is, tranquility. Since tranquility is the general principle governing all vicissitudes, it thus acquires its identity as the eternal. To follow the principle of tranquility, one should not take any reckless action. In applying this principle to both everyday life and political activities, he holds that non-action will become a panacea, for it runs no risk' (Ren, 1993: 30).

28.4 (Section 22)

To yield is yet to be preserved intact.
To be bent is yet to become straight.
To be hollow is yet to become full.
To be worn out is yet to be renewed.
To have little is yet to gain.
To have much is yet to be perplexed.
Therefore the sage holds on to the One
    And thus becomes a model for the world.
He does not cling to his ideas.
Therefore he is able to see things clearly.
He does not claim to be always right.
Therefore he is able to tell right from wrong.
He does not boast of himself.
Therefore he is given credit.
He does not think himself superior.
Therefore he is qualified for leadership.
It is only because he does not compete
    That the world cannot compete with him.
How could such an old saying be false
    As 'To yield is yet to be preserved intact?'

Truly one will be preserved wholly without going to the contrary.
This is a constant and natural precept.

Commentary

The first six lines in this section are assumed to be old sayings which pre-date Laozi. They take into consideration both the positive and negative aspects of almost all things and situations. Laozi uses them to reveal and justify his dialectical perspective, which is in fact recommended as a general principle in the treatment of social matters.

In everyday life, attention is often drawn to the outside of things rather than the inside of them. Thanks to his concrete experience and sharp observation, Laozi tends to contemplate and penetrate with insight social life and human activities. Thus he affirms that everything has two sides, which may be termed the positive and negative aspects. Both of them should be taken into account. Opposite as they are, they are interrelated and dependent upon one another, so they should be approached in respect of their interactions. For this reason, Laozi points out that the action of 'yielding' will lead to preservation intact; the tolerance of 'being bent' will lead to the advantage of becoming straight; the state of being 'hollow' will lead to the merit of becoming full; the state of being 'worn out' will lead to being renewed; and the situation of having 'little' will lead to more gains or greater achievements. In the final analysis, the *De* of non-competition (*bu zheng*) is concluded as the key to realizing all possible benefits. Being a code of conduct, it lies in the virtues of not clinging to one's ideas (*bu zi jian*), not claiming oneself to be always right (*bu zi shi*), and not boasting about oneself (*bu zi jin*). However, non-competition is obviously contrary to the competition that exists all around us. The interrelations between these two distinct strategies can also be observed from a dialectical and complementary viewpoint. Some things can be, as it were, accomplished by means of non-competition, whereas other things can only be accomplished by means of competition. It all depends on the specific situation. Hence, the way in which Laozi overemphasizes non-competition turns out to be lopsided or half-dialectical.

It is noteworthy that Laozi's advice 'to yield' and 'to be bent' is stemmed from his philosophy of keeping to the soft and the tender, which he regards as 'companions of life.' As for his notion of non-competition, it is the actual praxis of his principle of subsequent advance via initial retreat. He discusses elsewhere the importance of tenderness or softness, for he believes that 'the soft and the tender are companions of life' while 'the hard and the stiff are companions of death,' and accordingly, 'the tender and the weak stay in the superior position' while 'the hard and the strong fall in the inferior position' (see 11.2). Similarly, Laozi concludes that the tender and the weak can overcome the hard and the strong (see 11.3). As regards the necessity for and advantages of non-competition, he repeats it with reference to the *Dao* of Heaven, which he thinks does not compete and yet is good at winning (DDJ, Sect. 73). Thus he encourages people to model their behavior upon the *Dao* of Heaven. Consequently, if a person does not compete with others, nobody under Heaven can compete with him (DDJ, Sect. 66). This being the case, one should stay in an advantageous position if one is to fulfill one's wishes and hopes.

Laozi is so observant that he arrives at such a conclusion. That is, 'to have little is yet to gain.' This implies a steady and gradual progression of achievement. The greatest thing in the world begins, according to Laozi, with the minute or the little, and it grows bigger bit by bit. Hence, he advises people to start off by doing the minute or small in order to achieve the great or large. Some scholars interpret this sentence as 'to have little (knowledge) is yet to gain' (Ren, 1993: 37). I am inclined to hold that Laozi here talks about personal development in general from the perspective of the *Dao*.

Noticeably, the idea that 'the sage holds on to the One and thus becomes a model for the world' (*sheng ren bao yi wei tian xia shi*) is thought-provocating. By 'the One' is meant the *Dao* that Laozi advocates all along. It is assumed to mean 'taking the *Dao* (the One) as the instrument to observe destiny under Heaven.' The word *shi* does not only mean 'model.' It was also an instrument used in divination from the remote past to the Han Dynasty. The diviner tried to predict good or bad fortune by twirling this instrument. In this section, the *shi* that is used by the sage is not a material object, but the principle of the *Dao* (Ren, 1993: 37). Some scholars have this sentence as *sheng ren bao yi wei tian xia mu* based on the two Mawangdui DDJ versions unearthed in 1973. It is then rendered as: 'Therefore the sage who embraces the One will be able to govern the world' (Ai, 1993: 32–33). I think there is not much difference between these seemingly different interpretations in view of their hidden message.

28.5 (Section 13)

One is alarmed when in receipt of favor or disgrace.
One has great trouble because of one's body that he has.
What is meant by being alarmed by favor or disgrace?
Favor is regarded as superior, and disgrace as inferior.
One is alarmed when one receives them
    And equally alarmed when one loses them.
This is what is meant by being alarmed by favor or disgrace.
What is meant by having great trouble because of the body?
The reason why I have great trouble is that I have a body.
If I had no body,
    What trouble could I have?
Hence he who values the world in the same way as he values his body
    Can be entrusted with the world.
He who loves the world in the same way as he loves his body
    Can be entrusted with the world.

Commentary

In this section Laozi presents his thought of 'having no body' (*wu shen*), which can be viewed as identical with 'having no ego or self' (*wu ji*). 'The body' as such is considered the root cause of troubles and worries because it is symbolic of egoism or selfishness for self-preservation. As a matter of fact, it is only due to 'the body' that one is apt to be alarmed or depressed when receiving or losing favor or disgrace. This mentality underlines personal vanity and preoccupation with self-interest.

Judging from the context of the last four lines, we can conclude that Laozi thinks that the world can be a better place to live in if it is left to the selfless to govern. His idea of 'valuing the body' (*gui shen*) is presented in Section 44, in contrast to valuing such external things as material acquisitions, pleasure-snobbery, vanity, and reputation. Yet, his notion of 'having no body' (*wu shen*) is expressed in Sections 13 and 7 (DDJ) with reference to selfishness or egoism. That is why we need to be highly conscious of the different contexts involved.

According to Laozi, one will be able to make light of any favor or disgrace, and better still, be free from troubles or worries provided one rejects the body, or to be exact, eschews egoism. Having reached this stage of self-cultivation, one will surely, according to Laozi, attain the *Dao* as the supreme principle and act upon it accordingly, no matter what one is engaged in.

28.6 (Section 49)

The sage has no fixed mind of his own.
He takes the mind of the people as his mind.
I treat those who are good with goodness
    And I also treat those who are not good with goodness,
    Then everyone will try to become good.
I trust those who are trustworthy
    And I also trust those who are not trustworthy,
    Then everyone will try to become trustworthy.
When the sage governs the world,
    He seeks to put away his personal will
    And to help everyone return to the sphere of simplicity.
While the people all concentrate on their own eyes and ears,
    He renders them back to the sphere of infancy without desires

Commentary

This section reveals Laozi's political ideal exemplified by the lofty personality of the Daoist sage. Since he is selfless and rejects nobody, the sage is most liable to be well received and trusted by the people, thus establishing his moral influence over them. The probability of realizing this political ideal as well as cultivating this idealized personality is, in the final analysis, determined by such crucial virtues as selflessness and broad-mindedness. These virtues would in turn make it possible for the common people to return to 'the sphere of simplicity' or 'the sphere of infancy without desires.'

It should be stressed that the virtue of treating and trusting all people (with or without goodness) accounts for an important dimension of the sage's personality. This conduct of rejecting nobody as an idealized trait is also conclusively credited with remarkable consequences elsewhere. Take Section 62 (DDJ) for example. Laozi assumes that honored words can gain respect from others, and likewise, fine deeds can have an impact on others. 'Therefore the sage is always good at saving men, and consequently nobody is rejected. He is always good at saving things, and consequently nothing is rejected. This is called the hidden light' (see 13.2).

More significantly, Laozi seems to appreciate a kind of politics that is democratically people-oriented (Wang, 2009: 137–138). He therefore sets up the model of the sage 'who has no fixed mind of his own' and 'takes the mind of the people as his mind.' This means in modern terms that the sage ruler is not self-opinionated or self-centered such that he takes into due consideration of the public opinion. Nevertheless, it is always a big challenge for the rulers or leaders to make a sound judgment of the public opinion in terms of the common good from the past to the present.

28.7 (Section 48)

The pursuit of learning is to increase day after day.
The pursuit of the *Dao* is to decrease day after day.
It decreases and decreases again
　Till one gets to the point of take-no-action.
He takes no action and yet nothing is left undone.
In order to govern all under Heaven
　One should adopt the policy of doing nothing.
A person who likes to do anything arbitrary,
　Is not qualified to govern all under Heaven.

Commentary

This section makes a distinction between the pursuit of learning and that of the *Dao*. According to Laozi, the former leads to a continuous increase in practical knowledge associated with ambitions and desires, whereas the latter leads to a continuous increase in spiritual nourishment and freedom from desires. He who strives for more knowledge of such external things as social crafts is apt to have more ambitions and desires. Consequently, he will become enslaved and alienated with regard to his real self or genuine nature. In contrast, he who approaches the *Dao* will be steadily freed from these matters and able to return to simplicity as a kind of spiritual destination.

Once again, Laozi emphasizes the importance of take-no-action. He views it as a principle to be adopted by the ruler when conducting state affairs. At the same time he advises the ruler to model himself upon the Daoist sage by 'doing nothing' (*wu shi*) to disturb and control the people under his reign. Otherwise there will be no chance for him to become a qualified ruler and govern all under Heaven. This notion of Laozi in effect corresponds to his recommendation of 'self-transformation' (*zi hua*) to people in general.

'To do anything arbitrary' (*you shi*) is the implication of 'take-action' (*you wei*) in Laozi's terminology. It is considered to be negative and disadvantageous in the long run, contrasting sharply with 'doing nothing' or 'take-no-action.' It needs to be stressed that 'doing nothing' or 'take-no-action' simply means doing whatever does not disturb people or go against natural law. However, Laozi tends to absolutize the advantages of his favorite principle of 'take-no-(arbitrary or blind) action.' That is why it is taken more often than not as something extremely passive.

To sum up, naturalness or spontaneity is characteristic of the *Dao* of Heaven, which is assumed by Laozi to be the final standard or frame of reference for the *Dao* of human. The former is claimed to 'reduce whatever is excessive and supplement whatever is insufficient,' while the latter contrarily 'reduces the insufficient and offers more to the excessive' (see 5.1). Yet, the *Dao* of human will change into the *Dao* of the sage if it is modeled properly upon the *Dao* of Heaven. In this case it is 'to benefit all things and to cause no harm'; and correspondingly, it is 'to act for others but not to compete with them' (see 5.1).

With respect to 'take-no-action' as an essential feature of the *Dao*, it is so capable that it can leave nothing undone, as described in Sections 37, 38, 48, et al. (DDJ). Thus it plays an indispensable role in a political or social sense, because it can help rulers to subdue all things to their sway as a result of self-transformation. The importance of 'take-no-action' lies in the effect Laozi depicts in the following statements: 'I take no action and the people of themselves become transformed ... I disturb nobody and the people of themselves become prosperous' (see 21.1). Hopefully, the Daoist strategy would be practically working rather than wishful thinking in face of the hard times encountered nowadays. Or at least, it would provide a frame of reference for consideration in this regard. No matter what it would become of in itself, the fact is that DDJ has been read and reread in search of new messages and alternatives from the past to the present.

Appendix: The Dao De Jing of Laozi

Section 1 (see 1.1)

The *Dao* that can be told is not the constant *Dao*.
The Name that can be named is not the constant Name.
The Being-without-form is the origin of Heaven and Earth;
The Being-within-form is the mother of the myriad Things.
Therefore it is always from the Being-without-form
    That the subtlety of the *Dao* can be contemplated;
Similarly it is always from the Being-within-form
    That the manifestation of the *Dao* can be perceived.
These two have the same source but different names,
    They both may be called deep and profound.
The deepest and most profound
    Is the doorway to all subtleties.

Section 2 (see 12.1)

When the people of the world know the beautiful as beauty,
    There arises the recognition of the ugly.
When they know the good as good,
    There arises the recognition of the evil.

This is the reason why
    Have-substance and have-no-substance produce each other;
    Difficult and easy complete each other;
    Long and short contrast with each other;
    High and low are distinguished from each other;
    Sound and voice harmonize with each other;
    Front and back follow each other.

Thus, the sage conducts affairs through take-no-action;
    He spreads his doctrines through wordless teaching;

He lets all things grow without his initiation;
He nurtures all things but takes possession of nothing;
He promotes all things but lays no claim to his ability;
He accomplishes his work but takes no credit for his contribution.
It is because he takes no credit
   That his accomplishment stays with him for ever.

Section 3 (see 20.1)

Try not to exalt the worthy
   So that the people shall not compete.
Try not to value rare treasures,
   So that the people shall not steal.
Try not to display the desirable,
   So that the people's hearts shall not be disturbed.
Therefore the sage governs the people by
   Purifying their minds,
   Filling their bellies,
   Weakening their ambitions,
   And strengthening their bones.
He always keeps them innocent of knowledge and desires,
   And makes the crafty afraid to run risks.
He conducts affairs on the principle of take-no-action,
   And everything will surely fall into order.

Section 4 (see 1.2)

The *Dao* is empty (like a bowl),
   Its usefulness can never be exhausted?
The *Dao* is bottomless (like a valley),
   And is perhaps the ancestor of all things.
Invisible or formless, it appears non-existing
   But actually it exists.
I don't know whose child it is at all?
It seems to have even preceded the Lord.

Section 5 (see 2.4)

Heaven and Earth are not humane.
They regard all things as straw dogs.
The sage is not humane?

He regards all people as straw dogs.
The space between Heaven and Earth is like a bellows, isn't it?
While vacuous, it is never exhaustible.
When active, it turns out even more.
(To talk too much will surely lead to a quick demise.
Hence, it is better to keep to tranquility.)

Section 6 (see 1.3)

The spirit of the valley is immortal.
    It is called the subtle and profound female.
The gate of the subtle and profound female
    Is the root of Heaven and Earth.
It is continuous and everlasting,
    With a utility never exhausted.

Section 7 (see 27.1)

Heaven is eternal and Earth everlasting.
They can be so just because they do not exist for themselves.
And for this reason they can long endure.
Therefore the sage places himself in the background,
    But finds himself in the foreground
He puts himself away without self-consideration,
    And yet he always remains well-preserved.
It is because he has no personal interests
    That his personal interests are fulfilled.

Section 8 (see 14.1)

The supreme good is like water.
Water is good at benefiting all things
    And yet it does not compete with them.
It dwells in places that people detest,
    And thus it is so close to the *Dao*.
In dwelling, (the best man) loves where it is low.
In the mind, he loves what is profound
In dealing with others, he loves sincerity.
In speaking, he loves faithfulness.
In governing, he loves order.
In handling affairs, he loves competence.

In his activities, he loves timeliness.
Since he does not compete,
    He is free from any fault.

Section 9 (see 14.2)

To talk too much will lead to a quick demise.
Hence, it is better to keep to tranquility.
To keep what is full from overflowing
    Is not as good as to let it be.
If a sword-edge is sharpened to its sharpest,
    It will not be able to last long.
When your rooms are filled with gold and jade,
    You will not be able to keep them safe.
If you become arrogant because of honor and wealth,
    It will bring upon you misfortune.
Retreat as soon as the work is done.
Such is the *Dao* of Heaven.

Section 10 (see 28.1)

Can you keep the spirit and embrace the One
    Without departing from them?
Can you concentrate your vital force and achieve tenderness
    Like an infant without any desires?
Can you purify your mind and contemplate in depth
    Without any flecks?
Can you love the people and govern the state
    Without taking action?
Can you play the role of the feminine
    In the opening and closing of the gates of Heaven?
Can you understand all and penetrate all
    Without using your reasoning powers?

Section 11 (see 8.1)

Thirty spokes are united around the hub to make a wheel,
    But it is on the central hole for the axle
    That the utility of the chariot depends.
Clay is kneaded to mold a utensil,
    But it is on the empty space inside it
    That the utility of the utensil depends.

Doors and windows are cut out to form a room,
But it is on the interior vacancy
That the utility of the room depends.
Therefore, Have-substance brings advantage
While Have-no-substance creates utility.

Section 12 (see 10.1)

The five colors make one's eyes blind.
The five tones make one's ears deaf.
The five flavors dull one's palate.
Racing and hunting unhinge one's mind.
Goods that are hard to get tempt people to rob and steal.
Hence, the sage cares for the belly instead of the eyes;
And he rejects the latter but accepts the former.

Section 13 (see 28.5)

One is alarmed when in receipt of favor or disgrace.
One has great trouble because of one's body that he has.
What is meant by being alarmed by favor or disgrace?
Favor is regarded as superior, and disgrace as inferior.
One is alarmed when one receives them
And equally alarmed when one loses them.
This is what is meant by being alarmed by favor or disgrace.
What is meant by having great trouble because of the body?
The reason why I have great trouble is that I have a body.
If I had no body,
What trouble could I have?
Hence he who values the world in the same way as he values his body
Can be entrusted with the world.
He who loves the world in the same way as he loves his body
Can be entrusted with the world.

Section 14 (see 2.1)

You look at it but can not see it;
It is called the imageless.
You listen to it but can not hear it;
It is called the soundless.
You touch it but cannot find it;
It is called the formless.

These three cannot be further inquired into
  For they are the inseparable One.
The One is not bright when it is up,
  And not dark when it is down.
Infinite and indistinct, it cannot be named,
  Thus reverting to a state of non-thingness.

This is called shape without shape,
  Or image without image.
It is also called the Vague and the Elusive.
When meeting it, you cannot see its head.
When following it, you cannot see its back.
Hold on to the *Dao* of old,
  In order to harness present things.
From this you may know the primeval beginning.
This is called the law of the *Dao*.

Section 15 (see 26.1)

He who was adept at practicing the *Dao* in antiquity
  Was subtly profound and penetrating, too deep to be understood.
As he was beyond people's cognitive capacity,
  I can only describe him arbitrarily:
He was cautious, as if walking across a frozen river in winter;
He was vigilant, as if being threatened by an attack on all sides;
He was solemn and reserved, like a visiting guest;
He was supple and pliant, like ice about to melt;
He was broad, like the boundless sea;
He was vigorous, like the untiring blowing wind;
He was genuine and plain, like the uncarved block;
He was open and expansive, like a great valley;
He was merged and indifferent, like muddy water
Who could make the muddy gradually clear via tranquility?
Who could make the still gradually come to life via activity?
(It was nobody else but him.)
He who maintains the *Dao* does not want to be overflowing.
It is just because he does not want to be overflowing
  That he can be renewed when worn out.

Section 16 (see 28.3)

Try the utmost to get the heart into complete vacuity.
Be sure to keep the mind in steadfast tranquility.

All things are growing and developing
    And I see thereby their cycles
Though all things flourish with a myriad of variations,
    Each one eventually returns to its root.
This returning to its root is called tranquility;
This tranquility is called returning to its destiny;
Returning to its destiny is called the eternal.
To know the eternal is called enlightenment and wisdom.
Not to know the eternal is to take blind action,
    Thus resulting in disaster.
He who knows the eternal can embrace all.
He who embraces all can be impartial.
He who is impartial can be all-encompassing.
He who is all-encompassing can be at one with Heaven
He who is at one with Heaven can be at one with the *Dao*.
He who is at one with the *Dao* can be everlasting
    And free from danger throughout his life.

Section 17 (see 23.1)

The best kind of rulers are those whose existence
    Is merely known by the people below them.
The next-best are those who are loved and praised.
The next-best are those who are feared.
The next-best are those who are despised.
If trust in others is not sufficient,
    It will be unrequited.
(The best rulers) are cautious,
    And seldom issue orders.
When tasks are accomplished and affairs completed,
    The common people will say,
    'We simply follow the way of spontaneity'.

Section 18 (see 23.2)

When the great *Dao* is rejected,
    The doctrines of humanity and righteousness will arise.
When knowledge and craftiness appear,
    Great hypocrisy will also emerge.
When the six family relations are not in harmony,
    Filial piety and parental affection will be advocated.
When a country falls into chaos,
    Loyal ministers will be praised.

Section 19 (see 23.3)

Only when sageness is eliminated and craftiness discarded,
   Will people benefit a hundredfold.
Only when humanity is eradicated and righteousness abandoned,
   Will people return to filial piety and parental affection.
 Only when skill is thrown away and profit ignored,
   Will there be no more robbers or thieves.
Yet, these three are inadequate as a doctrine.
We therefore urge the following:
   Manifest plainness and embrace simplicity;
   Reduce selfishness and have few desires;
   And get rid of learning and have no worries.

Section 20 (see 26.2)

How much difference is there between ready approval
   And outright denunciation?
How much difference is there between good and evil?
What people fear cannot but be feared.
The multitude are merry, as if feasting on a day of sacrifice,
   Or as if ascending a tower to enjoy the scenery in springtime.
I alone remain tranquil and reluctant to distinguish.
I feel broad and far-reaching, as if at a loss;
I am indifferent and without concern,
   Like an infant that cannot smile;
I am wearied indeed,
   As if I have no home to return to.
The multitude are so brilliant and self-exhibiting,
   I alone seem to be lost in darkness and ignorance.
The multitude are so observant and discriminating,
   I alone intend to make no distinctions.
The multitude possess more than enough,
   I alone seem to lack everything.
The multitude have their reasons for taking action,
   I alone seem to be clumsy and incapable of nothing.
The multitude like to be endorsed and supported,
   I alone value the realization and attainment of the *Dao*.

Section 21 (see 2.3)

The character of the great *Dao*
   Follows from the *Dao* alone.

What is called the *Dao*
     Appears elusive and vague.
Vague and elusive as it is,
     There is the image in it.
Elusive and vague as it is,
     There is the real in it.
Profound und obscure as it is,
     There is the essence in it.
The essence is very concrete
     And contains the proof inside itself.
From the present back to the past
     Its name continues to ever last,
     By which alone we may know the beginning of all things.
How do I know their beginning as such?
Only through this.

Section 22 (see 28.4)

To yield is yet to be preserved intact.
To be bent is yet to become straight.
To be hollow is yet to become full.
To be worn out is yet to be renewed.
To have little is yet to gain.
To have much is yet to be perplexed.
Therefore the sage holds on to the One
     And thus becomes a model for the world.
He does not cling to his ideas.
Therefore he is able to see things clearly.
He does not claim to be always right.
Therefore he is able to tell right from wrong.
He does not boast of himself.
Therefore he is given credit.
He does not think himself superior.
Therefore he is qualified for leadership.
It is only because he does not compete
     That the world cannot compete with him.
How could such an old saying be false
     As 'To yield is yet to be preserved intact?'
Truly one will be preserved wholly without going to the contrary.
This is a constant and natural precept.

Section 23 (see 27.2)

A whirlwind does not last a whole morning;
A rainstorm does not last a whole day.
What causes them to be so? It is Heaven and Earth.
If Heaven and Earth cannot make them last long,
    How much less can man?
Therefore, he who seeks the *Dao* is identified with the *Dao*.
He who seeks the *De* is identified with the *De*.
He who seeks Heaven is identified with Heaven.
He who is identified with the *Dao*—
    The *Dao* is also happy to have him.
He who is identified with the *De*—
    The *De* is also happy to have him.
He who is identified with Heaven—
    Heaven is also happy to have him.

Section 24 (see 14.3)

He who stands on tiptoe is not steady.
He who doubles his stride cannot go far.
He who displays himself is not wise.
He who justifies himself is not prominent.
He who boasts of himself is not given any credit.
He who feels self-important is not fit for leadership.
From the perspective of the *Dao*,
    These are like remnants of food and tumors of the body,
    So disgusting that the one with the *Dao* stays away from them.
Likewise the sage knows himself but does not display himself.
He loves himself but does not feel self-important.
Hence he rejects that and accepts this.

Section 25 (see 1.4)

There was something undifferentiated and all-embracing
    That existed before Heaven and Earth.
Soundless and formless as it is,
    It depends on nothing external and stays inexhaustible.
    It operates with a circular motion and remains inextinguishable.
    It may be considered the mother of all under Heaven.
    I do not know its name, and hence call it the *Dao* far-fetchedly.
    If forced to give it another name, I shall call it the Great.

The Great is boundless and thus functioning everywhere.
It is functioning everywhere and thus becoming far-reaching.
It is becoming far-reaching and thus returning to the original point.
Therefore the *Dao* is great.
Heaven is great.
Earth is great.
And Man is also great.
There are four great things in the universe,
And Man is one of them.
Man follows the way of Earth.
Earth follows the way of Heaven.
Heaven follows the way of the *Dao*.
And the *Dao* follows the way of spontaneity.

Section 26 (see 20.2)

The heavy is the root of the light.
The tranquil is the lord of the hasty.
Therefore the sage travels all day
    Without leaving behind his baggage cart.
Although he enjoys a magnificent and comfortable life,
    He remains at leisure and without self-indulgence in it.
How is it that a king with ten thousand chariots
    Governs his kingdom so lightly and hastily?
Lightness is sure to lose the root.
Hastiness is sure to lose the lord.

Section 27 (See 27.3)

He who is adept at travelling leaves no track or trace behind.
He who is adept at speaking makes no blemishes or flaws.
He who is adept at counting uses no tallies or counters.
He who is adept at shutting the door needs no bolts,
    And yet it cannot be opened when shut.
He who is adept at binding things needs no strings,
    And yet they cannot be untied when bound.

Section 28 (see 28.2)

He who knows the masculine and keeps to the feminine
    Will become the ravine of the world

Being the ravine of the world,
    He will never depart from the constant *De*,
    But return to the state of infancy.
He who knows glory but keeps to disgrace
    Will become the valley of the world.
Being the valley of the world,
    He will be proficient in the constant *De*
    And return to the state of simplicity.
He who knows the white but keeps to the black
    Will become the principle of the world.
Being the principle of the world,
    He will possess the constant *De*
    And return to the state of ultimate infinity.
(When the simplicity is broken up,
    It is turned into vessels.
By using these vessels,
    The sage becomes the head of officials.
Hence a perfect government is not carved out of artificiality.)

Section 29 (see 9.2)

I think that one will not succeed
    When he desires to govern All under Heaven and act upon it.
All under Heaven as a sacred vessel should not be acted upon,
    Nor should it be held on to.
He who acts upon it will harm it.
He who holds on to it will lose it.
Thus the sage takes no action, and therefore fails in nothing.
He holds on to nothing and therefore loses nothing.

Of all the creatures some lead and some follow;
    Some breathe and some blow;
    Some are strong and some are weak;
    Some rise up and some fall down.
Hence the sage discards the extreme,
    The extravagant and the excessive.

Meanwhile, he desires to have no desires.
He does not value rare treasures.
He learns what is unlearned
He returns to what is missed.
Thus he helps all things in natural development,
    But does not dare to take any action.

Section 30 (see 22.1)

He who assists the ruler with the *Dao*
 Never seeks to dominate the world with military force.
The use of force is intrinsically dangerous:
Wherever armies are stationed,
 Briers and thorns grow wild.
As soon as great wars are over,
 Years of famine are sure to afflict the land.
Therefore an adept commander (of a defensive force) will
 Stop when he has achieved his aim.
He does not use force to dominate the world.
He achieves his aim but does not become arrogant.
He achieves his aim but does not boast about it.
He achieves his aim only because he has no other choice.
This is called achieving the aim without using force to dominate.
The strong and powerful rob and harm the old and weak.
This is called contrary to the *Dao*.
Whatever is contrary to the *Dao* will soon perish.

Section 31 (see 22.2)

Weapons are nothing but instruments of evil.
They are used only when there is no other choice.
Therefore, he who wins a battle is not praiseworthy.
If he thinks himself praiseworthy,
 He delights in the victory.
He who delights in the victory,
 Delights in the slaughter of men.
He who delights in the slaughter of men
 Will not succeed under Heaven.
For the multitude killed in the war,
 Let us mourn them with sorrow and grief.
For the victory won by force,
 Let us observe the occasion with funeral ceremonies.

Section 32 (see 4.2)

The *Dao* is eternal and has no name.
Though it is simple and seems minute,
 Nothing under Heaven can subordinate it.

If kings and lords were able to maintain it,
    All people would submit to them spontaneously.
Heaven and Earth unite to drip sweet dew,
    Without the command of men, it drips evenly over all.
Once a system comes into being,
    Names are instituted.
Once names are instituted,
    One has to know where and when to stop.
It is by knowing where and when to stop
    That one can be free from danger.
Everything under Heaven is embraced by the *Dao*,
    Just like every river or stream running into the sea.

Section 33 (see 15.1)

He who knows others is knowledgeable.
He who knows himself is wise.
He who conquers others is physically strong.
He who conquers himself is really mighty.
He who is contented is rich.
He who acts with persistence has a will.
He who does not lose his root will endure.
He who dies but is not forgotten enjoys longevity.

Section 34 (see 4.3)

The great *Dao* flows everywhere.
It may go left, it may go right.
All things rely on it for existence,
    And never does it turn away from them.
When it accomplishes its work,
    It does not claim credit for itself.
It preserves and nourishes all things,
    But it does not claim to be master over them.
Thus it may be called the minute.
All things come to it as to their home,
    Yet it does not act as their master.
Hence it may be called the great.
This is always the case with the sage
    Who is able to achieve his greatness
    Just because he himself never strives to be great.

Section 35 (see 2.2)

If you hold fast to the great image,
　All the people under Heaven will come to you.
They will come and do no harm to each other,
　But will all enjoy comfort, peace and health.
Music and dainties can make passers-by tarry,
　While the *Dao*, if spoken out, is insipid and tasteless.
Being looked at, it is imperceptible.
Being listened to, it is inaudible.
Being utilized, it is inexhaustible.

Section 36 (see 20.3)

In order to contract it,
　It is necessary to expand it first.
In order to weaken it,
　It is necessary to strengthen it first.
In order to destroy it,
　It is necessary to promote it first.
In order to grasp it,
　It is necessary to offer it first.
This is called subtle light.

The soft and the tender overcome the hard and the strong.
(Just as) fish should not be taken away from deep water,
　The sharp weapons of the state should not be displayed to the people.

Section 37 (see 9.1)

The *Dao* invariably takes no action,
　And yet there is nothing left undone.
If kings and lords are able to maintain it,
　All things will submit to them due to self-transformation.
If, after submission, they have resurging desires to act,
　I should subdue them by the nameless simplicity.
When they are subdued by the nameless simplicity,
　They will be free of desires.
Being free of desires, they will be tranquil,
　And the world will of itself be rectified.

Section 38 (see 6.2)

The man of the superior *De* is not conscious of his *De*
    And in this way he really possesses the *De*.
The man of the inferior *De* never loses sight of his *De*
    And in this way he has no true *De*.
The man of the superior *De* takes no action
    And thus nothing will be left undone.
The man of the inferior *De* takes action
    And thus something will be left undone.
The man of superior humanity takes action
    And so acts without purpose.
The man of superior righteousness takes action
    And so acts on purpose.
The man of superior propriety takes action,
    And when people do not respond to it,
    He will stretch out his arms and force them to comply.

Therefore, only when the *Dao* is lost does the *De* disappear.
Only when the *De* is lost does humanity appear.
Only when humanity is lost does righteousness appear.
Only when righteousness is lost does propriety appear.

Now propriety is a superficial expression of loyalty and faithfulness,
    And the beginning of disorder.
The man of foreknowledge has but the flower of the *Dao*
    And this is the beginning of ignorance.
Hence the great man dwells in the thick instead of the thin.
He dwells in the fruit instead of the flower.
Therefore he rejects the latter and accepts the former.

Section 39 (see 4.4)

Of those in the past that obtained the One
Heaven obtained the One and became clear;
The earth obtained the One and became tranquil;
The Gods obtained the One and became divine;
The Valleys obtained the One and became full;
All things obtained the One, and became alive and kept growing;
Kings and lords obtained the One and the world became peaceful.

Taking this to its logical conclusion we may say:
If Heaven had not thus become clear,
    It would soon have cracked;

If the earth had not thus become tranquil,
    It would soon have broken apart;
If the Gods had not thus become divine,
    They would soon have perished;
If the valleys had not thus become full,
    They would soon have dried up;
If all things had not thus become alive and kept growing,
    They would soon have become extinct;
If kings and lords had not thus become honorable and noble,
    They would soon have toppled and fallen.

It is always the case
    That the noble takes the humble as its root
    And the high takes the low as its base.
Hence kings and lords call themselves
    The orphaned, the solitary or the unworthy.
This is regarding the humble as the root of the noble.
    Is it not?
People disdain the 'orphaned,' 'solitary' or 'unworthy'.
And yet kings and lords call themselves by these terms.
Therefore the highest honor needs no flattering.
Thus with everything—
    Sometimes it may increase when decreased,
    And sometimes it may decrease when increased.
For this reason —
    They desire not to dazzle and glitter like jade,
    But to remain firm and plain like stone.

Section 40 (see 3.1)

Reversion is the movement of the *Dao*.
Weakness is the function of the *Dao*.
All things under Heaven come from Being-within-form.
And Being-within-form comes from Being-without-form.

Section 41 (see 25.1)

When the highest type of *literati* hear of the *Dao*,
    They diligently practice it.
When the average type of *literati* hear of the *Dao*,
    They half-believe it.
When the lowest type of *literati* hear of the *Dao*,
    They laugh heartily at it.

If they did not laugh at it,
    It would not be the *Dao*.

Therefore there is the established saying:
    The *Dao* that is bright seems to be dark;
    The *Dao* that advances seems to retreat;
    The *Dao* that is level seems to be uneven.
Thus the great *De* appears empty like a valley;
    The far-reaching *De* appears insufficient;
    The vigorous *De* appears inert;
    The simplistic *De* appears clumsy;
    The whitest appears soiled;
    The greatest square has no corners;
    The greatest vessel is unfinished;
    The greatest music sounds faint;
    The greatest form has no shape;
    The *Dao* is hidden and nameless.
Yet it is the *Dao* that initiates all things
    And brings them to completion.

Section 42 (see 4.1)

The *Dao* produces the One.
The One turns into the Two.
The Two give rise to the Three
The Three bring forth the myriad of things.
The myriad things contain Yin and Yang as vital forces,
Which achieve harmony through their interactions.

Section 43 (see 11.1)

The softest thing in the world
    Runs in and out of the hardest thing.
The invisible force penetrates any creviceless being.
Thereby I come to know the advantage of take-no-action.
Few in the world can realize the merits of wordless teaching
    And the benefits of doing nothing.

Section 44 (see 18.1)

Which is more dear, fame or life?
Which is more valuable, life or wealth?

Which is more detrimental, gain or loss?
Thus an excessive love of fame
    Is bound to cause an extravagant expense.
A rich hoard of wealth
    Is bound to suffer a heavy loss.
Therefore he who is contented will encounter no disgrace.
He who knows when and where to stop will meet no danger.
And in this way he can endure longer.

Section 45 (see 14.4)

What is most perfect seems to be incomplete,
    But its utility cannot be impaired.
What is most full seems to be empty,
    But its utility cannot be exhausted.
The most straight seems to be crooked.
The greatest skill seems to be clumsy.
The greatest eloquence seems to stutter.
The tranquil overcomes the hasty.
The cold overcomes the hot.
By remaining quiet and tranquil,
    One can become a model for all the people.

Section 46 (see 18.2)

When the world has the *Dao*,
    Warhorses are used in farming.
When the world lacks the *Dao*,
    Even mares in foal have to serve in battle.
There is no guilt greater than lavish desires.
There is no calamity greater than discontentment.
There is no defect greater than covetousness.
Therefore, he who is contented with knowing contentment
    Is always contented indeed.

Section 47 (see 15.2)

Without going out of the door
    One may know all-under-the-sky.
Without looking through the window
    One may see the *Dao* of Heaven.

The further one goes,
    The less one knows.
Therefore the sage knows without going about,
    Understands without seeing,
    And accomplishes without taking action.

Section 48 (see 28.7)

The pursuit of learning is to increase day after day.
The pursuit of the *Dao* is to decrease day after day.
It decreases and decreases again
    Till one gets to the point of take-no-action.
He takes no action and yet nothing is left undone.
In order to govern all under Heaven
    One should adopt the policy of doing nothing.
A person who likes to do anything arbitrary,
    Is not qualified to govern all under Heaven.

Section 49 (see 28.6)

The sage has no fixed mind of his own.
He takes the mind of the people as his mind.
I treat those who are good with goodness
    And I also treat those who are not good with goodness,
    Then everyone will try to become good.
I trust those who are trustworthy
    And I also trust those who are not trustworthy,
    Then everyone will try to become trustworthy.
When the sage governs the world,
    He seeks to put away his personal will
    And to help everyone return to the sphere of simplicity.
While the people all concentrate on their own eyes and ears,
    He renders them back to the sphere of infancy without desires

Section 50 (see 17.1)

Man comes alive into the world
    And goes dead into the earth.
Three out of ten will live longer.
Three out of ten will live shorter.
And three out of ten will strive for long life

But meet premature death.
And for what reason?
It is because of excessive preservation of life.
Only those who don't value their lives are wiser
Than those who overvalue their lives.

I have heard that those who are good at preserving life
    Will not meet rhinoceroses or tigers when traveling the byways,
    And will not be wounded or killed when fighting battles.
The rhinoceroses cannot butt their horns against them.
The tigers cannot fasten their claws upon them.
And weapons cannot thrust their blades into them.
And for what reason?
Because they are out of the range of death

Section 51 (see 6.1)

The *Dao* begets all beings,
    And the *De* fosters them.
Substance gives them physical forms,
    And the environment completes them.
Therefore all beings venerate the *Dao* and honor the *De*.
As for the veneration of the *Dao* and the honoring of the *De*,
    It is not out of obedience to any orders;
    It comes spontaneously due to their naturalness.
Hence the *Dao* begets all beings,
    And the *De* fosters them, rears them and develops them,
    Matures them and makes them bear fruit,
    Protects them and helps them breed.
To produce them without taking possession of them,
    To raise them without vaunting this as its own merit,
    And to nourish them without controlling them,
    This is called the Profound *De*.

Section 52 (see 15.3)

There was a beginning of the universe,
    Which may be called the mother of the universe.
He who has found the mother
    Thereby understands her sons.
He who has understood the sons
    And still keeps to the mother

Will be free from danger throughout his life.
Block up the holes;
   Shut up the doors;
   And till the end of life there will be no toil.
Open the holes;
   Meddle with affairs;
   And till the end of life there will be no salvation.
Seeing what is small is called enlightenment.
Keeping to weakness is called strength.
Use the light.
Revert to enlightenment.
And thereby avoid danger to one's life—
   This is called practicing the eternal.

Section 53 (see 10.2)

If I have a little wisdom,
   I will walk along a broad way
   And fear nothing but going astray.
The broad way is very even,
   But the powerful delight in by-paths.
The courts are exceedingly corrupt,
   Whereas the fields are exceedingly weedy
   And the granaries are exceedingly empty.
They are wearing elegant clothes,
   Carrying sharp swords,
   Enjoying exquisite food and drink,
   And owning abundant wealth and treasures.
They can be called robber chieftains.
This is surely against the *Dao*.

Section 54 (see 7.1)

He who is good at building cannot be shaken.
He who is good at holding can lose nothing.
Thus his ancestral sacrifice can pass down
   From generation to generation.
When cultivated and exercised in the person,
   The *De* will become pure and genuine.
When cultivated and exercised in the family,
   The *De* will become full and overflowing.
When cultivated and exercised in the common,

The *De* will become constant and everlasting.
When cultivated and exercised nationwide,
   The *De* will become powerful and abundant.
When cultivated and exercised worldwide,
   The *De* will become universal and widespread.

Therefore, (by taking it as a standard should we)
   Use this person to examine other persons,
   Use this family to examine other families,
   Use this community to examine other communities,
   Use this country to examine other countries.
   And use this world to examine other worlds.
How do I know the situation of all things under Heaven?
Precisely by the method above-mentioned.

Section 55 (see 7.2)

He who possesses the *De* in abundance
   Can be compared to a newborn infant.
Poisonous insects will not sting him.
Fierce brutes will not injure him.
Birds of prey will not attack him.
His bones are weak and his sinews tender,
   But his grasp is firm.
He does not yet know about the intercourse of male and female.
   But his organ is aroused
   For his physical essence is at its height.
He may cry all day without becoming hoarse,
   For his innate harmony is simply perfect.
The essence and harmony as such are natural and constant.
To know this is called being wise.
The desire to multiply life's enjoyments means ill omen
The mind to employ vital energy excessively suffers fatal stiffness.
Things that have grown strong commence to become old.
This is called 'being contrary to the *Dao*'.
Whatever is contrary to the *Dao* will soon perish.

Section 56 (see 15.4)

He who knows does not speak,
   He who speaks does not know.
He blocks the vent,

Closes the door,
Blunts the sharpness,
Unties the tangles,
Softens the glare,
And mixes with the dust.
This is called Profound Identification.

Therefore people cannot get intimate with him,
　Nor can they estrange themselves from him.
People cannot benefit him,
　Nor can they harm him.
People cannot ennoble him,
　Nor can they debase him.
　For this reason he is esteemed by all-under-Heaven.

Section 57 (see 21.1)

A state should be governed in a normal way.
An army should be operated in an unusual way.
The world should be administered by doing nothing.
How do I know that it should be so?
Through the following:
The more prohibitive enactments there are in the world,
　The poorer the people will become;
The more sharp weapons men have,
　The more troubled the state will be;
The more crafts and techniques men possess,
　The more vicious things will appear;
The more laws and orders are made prominent,
　The more robbers and thieves will spring up.
Therefore the sage says:
'I take no action and the people of themselves become transformed.
I love tranquility and the people of themselves become righteous.
I disturb nobody and the people of themselves become prosperous.
I have no desires and the people of themselves become simple'.

Section 58 (see 16.1)

When the government is generous and non-discriminatory,
　The people will remain honest and sincere;
When the government is severe and discriminatory,
　The people will become crafty and cunning.

Misfortune is that beside which fortune lies;
    Fortune is that beneath which misfortune lurks.
Who knows what may be their ultimate cause?
There is no fixed and normal frame of reference.
The normal can suddenly turn into the abnormal.
The good can suddenly turn into the evil.
The people have been deluded for a long time.

Therefore, the sage is as pointed as a square, but never stays stiff;
He is as sharp as a knife, but never cuts anybody;
He is frank and straightforward, but never aggressive;
He is bright and shining, but never dazzling.

Section 59 (see 20.4)

To rule people and to serve Heaven
    Nothing is better than the principle of frugality.
Only by frugality can one get ready early.
To get ready early means to accumulate the *De* continuously.
With the continuous accumulation of the *De*,
    One can overcome every difficulty.
If one can overcome every difficulty,
    He will then acquire immeasurable capacity.
With immeasurable capacity,
    He can achieve the *Dao* to govern the country.
He who has the *Dao* of the country can maintain sovereignty.
This is called the way in which the roots are planted deep,
    And the stalks are made firm;
    Longevity is achieved,
    And sovereignty is made everlasting.

Section 60 (see 20.5)

Governing a large country is like cooking a small fish.
If the *Dao* is applied to the world,
    Ghosts will lose their supernatural influence.
It is not that they will actually lose it,
    But that their influence will no longer be able to harm men.
It is not that their influence will no longer be able to harm men,
    But that the sage also will not harm men.
Since these two do not harm men, and vice versa,
    They all enjoy peaceful co-existence.

Section 61 (see 20.6)

Governing a large country is like lying in a lower place.
This country may be likened to rivers and streams
    Flowing into the sea.
It lies lower such that all in the world runs to it.
It is the converging point of all in the world.
It is the female of the world
    That always overcomes the male via tranquility
    And with tranquility she lies lower.
Hence a big state can rally small states around it
    If it lowers itself to them.
Small states can win trust from a big state
    If they lower themselves to it.
Thus a big state can rally small states by lowering itself.
Small states can win trust from a big state by lowering themselves.
What a big state wants is to unite and lead small states.
What small states want is to be rallied and protected by the big state.
When both sides get what they respectively want,
The big state should learn to keep itself lower.

Section 62 (see 13.2)

The *Dao* is the storehouse of all things.
It is treasured by the good man,
    And also preserved by the bad man.

Honored words can gain respect from others.
Fine deeds can have an impact on others.
Even if a man is bad,
    Why should he be ever rejected?
Therefore the sage is always good at saving men,
    And consequently nobody is rejected.
He is always good at saving things,
    And consequently nothing is rejected.
This is called the hidden light.
Therefore, the good man is the teacher of the bad.
And the bad is the material from which the good may learn.
He who does not value the teacher
    Or care for the material,
    Will still be greatly deluded
    Though he thinks himself clever.
Such is called the significant subtlety of the *Dao*.

Therefore, on the occasion of enthroning an emperor
    Or installing the three ministers,
    It is better to offer the *Dao* as a present
    Though there are grand ceremonies of saluting them
    With the round jadeware, followed by the four-horse chariot.

Why did the ancients value this *Dao* so much?
Did they not say, 'Those who seek shall attain and
    Those who sin shall be freed?'
For this reason it is valued by all under Heaven.

Section 63 (see 19.1)

Consider take-no-action as a code of conduct.
Consider make-no-trouble as a way of deed.
Consider have-no-flavor as a method of taste.

It is a rule in the world that
    The most difficult things begin with the easy ones,
    And the largest things arise from the minute ones
Hence, tackle the difficult while it is still easy;
    Achieve the large while it is still minute.
For this reason, the sage never strives for the great,
    And thereby he can accomplish it.

He who makes promises too readily will surely lack credibility.
He who takes things too easily will surely encounter difficulties.
Therefore, even the sage regards things as difficult,
    And he is free from difficulties as a result.

Section 64 (see 19.2)

What is stable is easy to hold.
What is not yet manifest is easy to handle.
What is brittle is easy to disintegrate.
What is minute is easy to eliminate.
Deal with matters before they occur.
Put them in order before disorder arises.
A tree as huge as one's embrace grows from a tiny shoot.
A tower of nine stories rises from a heap of earth.
A journey of a thousand miles starts from the first step.
People often fail when they are on the point of success

In their conduct of affairs.
If they remain still as careful at the end as at the beginning,
    They will never suffer failures.

Section 65 (see 23.4)

In ancient times he who practiced the *Dao* well
    Did not use it to enlighten the people.
Instead he used it to make them simple.
Now the people are difficult to govern
    Because they have too much craftiness.
Thus, governing a country by craftiness is a disaster for it.
And not governing it by craftiness is a blessing for it.
He who knows these two also knows the principle.
It is called the profound *De* to always know the principle.
The Profound *De* is deep and far-reaching;
It returns to the origin with all things,
    And then leads to the great naturalness.

Section 66 (see 20.7)

The great rivers and seas can be the kings of the mountain streams
    Because they skillfully stay below them.
That is why they can be their kings.
Therefore, in order to be above the people,
    The sage must place himself below them in his words.
In order to be ahead of the people,
    He must place himself behind them in his person.
In this way, the sage is above the people,
    But they do not feel his weight.
He is ahead of the people,
    But they do not feel his hindrance
Therefore the whole world delights in praising him
    And never gets tired of him.
Simply because he does not compete with others,
    Nobody under Heaven can compete with him.

Section 67 (see 10.3)

I have three treasures
    Which I grasp and keep.

The first is 'kindness'.
The second is 'frugality'.
The third is 'to dare not be ahead of the world'.

With kindness, one can become courageous.
With frugality, one can become generous.
With not daring to be ahead of the world,
    One can become the leader of the world.

Now it is a fatal mistake
    To seek courage by abandoning kindness,
    To seek generosity by abandoning frugality,
    And to seek precedence by abandoning retreat.
With kindness, one can be victorious in the case of attack,
    And remain firm in the case of defense.
Heaven will help and protect such a one through kindness.

Section 68 (see 21.2)

In the past—
An adept commander did not display his martial prowess.
An adept warrior did not become angry.
An adept conqueror did not tussle with his enemy.
An adept manager of men placed himself below them.
This is called the virtue of non-competition.
This is called the use of others' force.
This is called the supreme principle of matching Heaven.

Section 69 (see 21.3)

In the past, a military strategist said:
'I dare not take the offensive, but I take the defensive.
I dare not advance an inch, but I retreat a foot'.
This means (to make the invading force):
    Advancing onward without battle formation,
    Raising his arm without morale enhancement,
    Holding his weapons without normal function,
    And tackling the enemy without meeting him.
There is no greater disaster than underestimating the enemy.
Such underestimation is tantamount to self-abandonment.
Therefore, when two well-matched armies clash in battle,
    It is the side which retreats first that will win.

Section 70 (see 25.2)

All the world says that my *Dao* is great,
   But it does not resemble anything concrete.
Just because it is great,
   It does not resemble anything concrete.
It would have been small for long if it did.

My words are very easy to understand and practice.
But no one in the world can understand and practice them.
My words have their own source.
My deeds have their own master.

It is merely because people do not know this
   That they fail to understand me.
Those who can understand me are very few,
   And those who can follow me are hard to meet.
Therefore the sage wears coarse garb,
   But conceals a precious jade in his bosom.

Section 71 (see 15.5)

It is best to know that you don't know.
It is an aberration to pretend to know when you don't know.
The sage is free from this aberration
   Because he recognizes it as such.
He can be free from this aberration
   Only when he recognizes it as such.

Section 72 (see 20.8)

When people do not fear the power of the ruler,
   Something terribly dreadful will take place.
Do not force the people out of their dwellings.
Do not exploit the people to the point that they cannot live.
They will not detest and overthrow the regime
Only when they are not excessively oppressed.

Section 73 (see 20.9)

He who is brave in daring will be killed.
He who is brave in not daring will survive.

Of these two kinds of bravery,
    One is advantageous, while the other is harmful.
Heaven detests what it detests.
Who knows its cause?
The *Dao* of Heaven does not compete, and yet it is good at winning.
It does not speak, and yet it is good at responding.
It is not called, and yet it comes along on its own.
It is frankly at ease, and yet it plans well.
The net of Heaven is large and vast,
    It lets nothing escape, despite its wide meshes.

Section 74 (see 20.10)

If the people are not afraid of death,
    What is the point of trying to frighten them with death?
In order to make people always afraid of death,
    We can catch and kill the trouble-makers.
Then, who will dare to make trouble?
There is always a master in charge of executions.
To carry out executions in place of the master
    Is like hewing wood in place of a skillful carpenter.
Of those who hew wood in place of the carpenter,
    Very few escape cutting their own hands.

Section 75 (see 20.11)

The people suffer from famine
    Because the ruler levies too much tax-grain.
Thus they suffer from famine.
The people are difficult to rule
    Because the ruler too often takes action.
Thus they are difficult to rule.
The people take life lightly
    Because the ruler longs for life so avidly.
Thus they take life lightly.

Section 76 (see 11.2)

When alive, man is soft and tender.
After death, he is hard and stiff.

All things like grass and trees are soft and tender when alive,
    Whereas they become withered and dried when dead.
Therefore, the hard and the stiff are companions of death
    Whereas the soft and the tender are companions of life.
Hence an army will be shattered when it becomes strong.
A tree will be broken when it grows huge.
The hard and the strong fall in the inferior position;
The soft and the tender stay in the superior position.

'The violent and the strong do not die natural deaths'.
I shall take this principle as the father of my teaching.

Section 77 (see 5.1)

Does not the *Dao* of Heaven resemble the drawing of a bow?
When the string is taut, press it down.
When it is low, raise it up.
When it is excessive, reduce it.
When it is insufficient, supplement it.
The *Dao* of Heaven reduces whatever is excessive
    And supplements whatever is insufficient.
The *Dao* of human does the opposite.
It reduces the insufficient,
    And adds more to the excessive.
Who is able to have a surplus to offer to the world?
Only the one who has the *Dao*.
The sage does not accumulate for himself.
The more he shares with others, the more he possesses.
The more he gives to others, the richer he becomes.
The *Dao* of Heaven benefits all things and causes no harm.
The *Dao* of the sage acts for others but never competes with them.

Section 78 (see 11.3)

Nothing in the world is softer and weaker than water,
    But no force can compare with it in attacking the hard and the strong.
For this reason there is no substitute for it.
Everyone in the world knows
    That the soft can overcome the hard,
    And the weak can overcome the strong,
    But none can put it into practice.

Therefore the sage says;
'He who shoulders the disgrace for his nation
   Can be the sovereign of the country;
   He who bears the misfortune of his nation
   Can be the king of the world'.
Positive words seem to be their opposite.

Section 79 (see 5.2)

To reconcile two sides in deep hatred
   Is surely to leave some hatred behind.
If one returns good for evil
   How can this be taken as a proper solution?
Therefore the sage keeps the counterfoil of the tally,
   Yet he does not demand payment of the debt.
The virtuous man is as kind and generous as the tally keeper
   While the non-virtuous is as harsh and calculating as a tax collector.
The *Dao* of Heaven has no preference.
It is constantly with the good man.

Section 80 (See 24.1)

Let there be a small state with few people.
It has various kinds of instruments,
   But let none of them be used.
Let the people not risk their lives, and not migrate far away.
Although they have boats and carriages,
   Let there be no occasion to ride in them.
Although they have armor and weapons,
   Let there be no occasion to display them.
Let the people return to knotting cords and using them.
Let them relish their food,
   Beautify their clothing,
   Feel comfortable in their homes
   And delight in their customs.
Although the neighboring states are within sight of one another,
   And the crowing of cocks and the barking of dogs
   On both sides can be heard,
   Their peoples may die of old age without even meeting each other.

Section 81 (see 13.1)

True words are not beautiful.
Beautiful words are not true.
A good man is not an eloquent arguer.
An eloquent arguer is not a good man.
He who knows does not show off his extensive learning.
He who shows off his extensive learning does not know.

References

Works in English

Baynes, Carry F. (tr.) (1980), *The I Ching or Book of Changes*. New Jersey: Princeton University Press.

Chan, Wing-tsit (tr. and ed.) (1973), *A Source Book in Chinese Philosophy*. New Jersey: Princeton University Press.

Confucius. (1983), *The Analects*. (tr. D. C. Lau). London: Penguin.

Fung, Yu-lan (tr.) (1952), *A History of Chinese Philosophy*, vol. 1. New York: Columbia University Press.

—— (1989), *A Taoist Classic: Chuang Tzu*. Beijing: Foreign Languages Press.

—— (1991), *Selected Philosophical Writings*. Beijing: Foreign Languages Press.

Gong, Dafei and Feng, Yu (eds) (1994), *Chinese Maxims*. Beijing: Sinolingua.

Graham, A. C. (1989), *Disputers of the Tao*. Illinois: Open Court Publishing Company.

Henricks, Robert G. (tr.) (1990), *Lao-tzu Te-Tao Ching*. London: The Bodley Head.

Kiu, K. L. (ed.) (1991), *100 Ancient Chinese Fables*. Beijing: Foreign Languages Press.

Lau, D. C. (tr.) (1979), *Lao Tzu: Tao Te Ching*. London: Penguin.

Legge, James (tr.) (1995), *Book of Changes*. Changsha: Hunan Press.

Li, Zehou (1994), *The Path of Beauty*. (tr. Gong Lizeng). Oxford: Oxford University Press.

—— (2006), *Four Essays on Aesthetics*. Lanham: Lexington Books.

—— (2010), *The Chinese Aesthetic Tradition*. (tr. Maija Bell Samei). Honolulu: Hawaii University Press.

Liu, Xie (2003), *Dragon-carving and the Literary Mind*. (tr. Yang Guobin). Beijing: Foreign Language Teaching and Research Press.

Lynn, Richard John (tr.) (1994), *I Ching: The Classic of Changes*. New York: Columbia University Press.

—— (tr.) (1999), *Tao-te ching: The Classic of the Way and Virtue*. New York: Columbia University Press.

Ren, Jiyu (ed.) (1993), *A Taoist Classic: The Book of Lao Zi*. (trs. He Guanghu et al.). Beijing: Foreign Languages Press.

Schwartz, Benjamin I. (1985), *The World of Thought in Ancient China*. Cambridge, MA: Harvard University Press.

Sunzi (1993), *The Art of War*. Beijing: Military Sciences Press.

Waley, Arthur (tr.) (1994), *The Way and Its Power*. Changsha: Hunan Press.

Wang, Keping (1998), *The Classic of the Dao: A New Investigation*. Beijing: Foreign Languages Press.

—— (2009), *Chinese Way of Thinking*. Shanghai: Brilliant Books.

Wang, Rongpei (tr.). (1999), *Zhuangzi*. Beijing: Foreign Languages Press.

Waston, Burton (tr.) (1968), *The Complete Works of Chuang Tzu*. New York: Columbia University Press.

Works in Chinese

Ai, Qi (ed.) (1993), *Laozi bashiyi zhang* (*81 Sections of the Dao De Jing of Laozi*). Tianjin: Tianjin Academy of Social Sciences Publishing House.

Beida, Zhexuexi (ed.) (1980), *Zhongguo zhexue shi* (*A History of Chinese Philosophy*, vol. 1. Beijing: Zhonghua Shuju.

Cao, Lihua (1994), *Zhonghua chuantrong meixue tixi tanyuan* (*An Investigation into the Origin of Chinese Traditional Aesthetics*). Beijing: Capital Normal University Press.

Chen, Guying (1983), *Zhuangzi jin zhu jin yi* (*The Works of Zhuangzi Newly Annotated*). Beijing: Zhonghua Shuju.

—— (1992), *Lao Zhuang xin lun* (*New Essays on Laozi and Zhuangzi*). Shanghai: Shanghai Zhongguo Guji Press.

—— (1992), *Laozi zhuyi ji pingjie* (*The Dao De Jing of Laozi Annotated and Commented*). Beijing: Zhonghua Shuju.

Dai, Jianye (1993), *Laozi: Zi ran ren sheng* (*Laozi: A Natural Life*). Wuhan: Changjiang Wenyi Press.

Fang, Dongmei (2005), *Zhongguo zzhexue jingshen jiqi fazhan* (*The Spirit of Chinese Philosophy and its Development*, vols 1–2), tr. Sun Zhishen. Taipei: Liming Wenhua.

Feng, Dawen (1992), *Hui gui zi ran: Dao jia de zhu diao yu bianzou* (*Return to Nature: The Main Tone and Variation of Daoism*). Guangzhou: Guangdong Renmin Press.

Feng, Qi (1993), *Zhongguo gudai zhexue de luoji fazhan* (*A Logical Development of Ancient Chinese Philosophy*). Shanghai: Shanghai Renmin Press.

Feng, Tianyu (1994), *Zhonghua yuandian jingshen* (*The Spirit of Chinese Meta-Classics*). Shanghai: Shanghai Renmin Press.

Fung, Yu-lan (Feng Youlan) (1992), *Zhongguo zhexue shi xinbian* (*New History of Chinese Philosophy*, vol. 2). Beijing: Renmin Press.

Gao, Heng (1988), *Laozi zheng gu* (*The Book of Laozi Revised and Annotated*). Beijing: Zhongguo Shudian.

Gao, Ming (1996), *Boshu Laozi jiaozhu* (*The Mawangdui Version of the Dao De Jing Revised and Annotated*), Beijing: Zhonghua Shuju.

Gao, You (ed.) (1986), *Huainanzi zhu* (*The Book of Huannanzi Annotated*). Shanghai: Shanghai Shudian.

Ge, Rongjin (ed.) (1991), *Dao jia wenhua yu xian dai wen ming* (*Daoist Culture and Modern Civilization*). Beijing: Chinese Renmin University Press.

Gu, Di and Guan, Tong (2009), *Laozi shi jiang* (*Ten Lectures on the Dao De Jing of Laozi*). Shanghai: Shanghai Renmin Press.

Gu, Di and Zhou, Ying (1991), *Laozi tong* (*A comprehensive Study of the Dao De Jing of Laozi*), vols 1–2. Changchun: Jinlin Renmin Press.

Guo, Yi (2001), *Guodian zhujian yu xianqin xueshu sixiang* (*Guodian Excavated Texts on Bamboo Slips and Pre-Qin Scholarly Thoughts*). Shanghai: Shanghai Education Press.

Han, Feizi (1984), *Jie Lao* (*Understanding Laozi*), in *Zhongguo zhexue shi ziliao xuanji* (*Selected Sources of the History of Chinese Philosophy*, Pre-Qin Period, vol. 3). Beijing: Zhonghua Shuju, pp. 1252–1283.

He, Yirong (1996), *Dao De Jing zhuyi yu xijie* (*The Dao De Jing Annotated and Analyzed*). Tianjin: Baihua Wenyi Press.

Heshang, Gong (ed.) (1991), *Dao de zhen jing* (*A True Classic: Dao De Jing*). Shanghai: Shanghai Zhongguo Guji Press.

Jiang, Xichang (ed.) (1988), *Laozi jiaogu* (*The Dao De Jing of Laozi Revised and Annotated*). Chengdu: Chengdu Guji Press.

Li, Zehou (1986), *Zhongguo gudai sixiang shi lun* (*Essays on the History of Ancient Chinese Thoughts*). Beijing: Renmin Press.

—— (1989), *Huaxia meixue* (*Chinese Aesthetics*). Beijing: Guoji Wenhua Jiaoliu Press.

Li, Zehou and Liu, Gangji (eds) (1984), *Zhongguo meixue shi* (*A History of Chinese Aesthetics*), vol. 1. Beijing: China Social Sciences Press.

Liu, Xiaogan (2006), *Laozi gujin* (*The Dao De Jing of Laozi: From the Past to the Present*, vols 1–2). Beijing: China Social Sciences Press.

Ma, Xulun (ed.) (1956), *Laozi jiaogu* (*The Dao De Jing of Laozi Revised and Annotated*). Beijing: Beijing Guji Press.

Qiao, Changlu (1990), *Zhongguo rensheng zhexue* (*Chinese Philosophy of Life*). Beijing: Chinese Renmi University Press.

Qin, Xincheng and Liu, Shengyuan. (1993), *Laozi zhuan* (*A Biography of Laozi*). Shijiazhuang: Huashan Wenyi Press.

Ren, Jiyu (ed.) (1963), *Zhongguo zhexue shi* (*A History of Chinese Philosophy*, vol. 1). Beijing: Renmin Press.

Sha, Shaohai (ed.) (1992), *Laozi quanyi* (*A Complete Paraphrase of the Dao De Jing of Laozi*). Guiyang: Guizhou Renmin Press.

Sima, Qian (1992), *Shi ji* (*Historical Records*). Changsha: Yuelu Press.

Sun, Yikai et al. (1992), *Laozi wai zhuan Laozi baiwen* (*A Story of Laozi and 100 Questions on His Ideas*). Hefei: Anhui Renmin Press.

Wang, Anshi (ed.) (1982), *Dao De Jing zhu* (*The Dao De Jing Annotated*), in *Zhongguo zhexue shi ziliao xuanji* (*Selected Sources of the History of Chinese Philosophy*, Song-Yuan-Ming Periods, vol. 2). Beijing: Zhonghua Shuju, pp. 171–181.

Wang, Bi (ed.) (1989), *Laozi zhu* (*The Dao De Jing of Laozi Annotated*). Shanghai: Shanghai Zhongguo Guji Press.

Wang, Meng (2009), *Laozi shiba jiang* (*18 Lectures on the Dao De Jing of Laozi*). Beijing: Sanlian Shudian.

Wang, Ming (1987), *Dao jia he Dao jia sixiang yanjiu* (*A Study of Daoism and Its Ideas*). Beijing: China Social Sciences Press.

Xu, Fuguan (1987), *Zhongguo yishu jingshen* (*The Spirit of Chinese Art*). Shengyang: Chunfeng Wenyi Press.

Xu, Kangsheng (1993), *Laozi yu Dao jia* (*Laozi and Daoism*). Beijing: Xinhua Press.

Ye, Lang (1987), *Zhongguo meixue shi dagang* (*An Outline of the History of Chinese Aesthetics*). Shanghai: Shanghai Renmin Press.

Yin, Zhenhuan (2001), *Chu jian Laozi bianxi* (*The Guodian Bamboo Version of the Dao De Jing Identified and Analyzed*), Beijing: Zhonghua Shuju.

Zhang, Dainian (1982), *Zhongguo zhexue dagang* (*An Outline of Chinese Philosophy*). Beijing: China Social Sciences Press.

Zhang, Songru (ed.) (1987), *Laozi jiaoshuo* (*The Dao De Jing of Laozi Revised and Commented*). Jinan: Qilu Shushe.

Zhang, Wenxun (1988), *Ru Dao Shi meixue sixiang tansuo* (*An Inquiry into the Aesthetic Ideas in Confucianism, Daoism and Buddhism*). Beijing: China Social Sciences Press.

Zhang Yucai (ed.) (1988), *Daode xuanjing yuanzhi xu* (Preface to *The Fundamentals of the Dao De Jing*), in *Daozang* (*Collection of Daoist Scriptures*, Beiijing: Wenwu Press.

Zhu, Daxing (2007), *Dunhuang ben Laozi yanjiu* (*A Study of the Tunhuang Edition of the Dao De Jing of Laozi*). Beijing: Zhonghua Shuju.

Zhu, Qianzhi (1984), *Laozi jiaoshi* (*The Dao De Jing Revised and Annotated*). Beijing: Zhonghua Shuju.

Index